United Kingdom Travel Guide 2024-2025

Discover Iconic Landmarks, Cultural Experiences, and Hidden Gems Across the UK

Emily Hawthorne

INTRODUCTION 9
   Welcome to the United Kingdom 9
   Why Visit the UK in 2024-2025? 11
   How to Use This Guide 13

CHAPTER 1 15
Getting To The United Kingdom 15
   International Flights 15
   Entry Requirements and Visas 18
   Best Times to Visit 19
   Travel Insurance 21
   Health and Safety 22

CHAPTER 2 23
Exploring the Regions of the UK 23
   England: History, Culture, and Vibrant Cities. 23

   Scotland: Highlands, Castles, and Traditions.. 26

   Wales: Natural Beauty and Coastal Adventures 28

   Northern Ireland: Ancient History and Modern Culture 30

CHAPTER 3..32
Top Attractions and Must-See Sights............32
   London's Icons...32
   Historic Sites Across England...................... 34
   Scotland's Historic and Natural Wonders.... 36
   Wales' Natural and Historical Highlights.... 38
   Northern Ireland's Unique Attractions........ 40

CHAPTER 4..42
Cultural Experiences Across the UK............ 42
   The British Museum and Other World-Class Museums..42
   Music, Festivals, and Events........................45
   Theatre and the Arts in London's West End 47
   Music Festivals Across the UK.................... 50
      Glastonbury Festival................................50
      Reading and Leeds Festivals................... 51
      The Isle of Wight Festival....................... 52
      Creamfields...53
      Glastonbury Festival of Contemporary Performing Arts....................................... 54
      The Secret Garden Party.........................55

    South West Four..56

    The Great Escape...57

CHAPTER 5.. 59

Culinary Journey: Exploring British Food and Drink.. 59

    Traditional British Cuisine...........................59

    Afternoon Tea and British Pubs...................61

    Local Delicacies from Each Region............ 62

    Local Restaurant Tips.................................. 65

    Local Restaurant Insights.............................67

        London...67

        Edinburgh... 69

        Cardiff...70

        Belfast... 71

CHAPTER 6.. 73

Outdoor and Adventure Activities.................... 73

    Hiking in the Scottish Highlands and Lake District.. 73

    Coastal Walks and National Parks............... 75

    Wildlife Watching and Outdoor Adventures... 77

    Adventure Activities 79
    UK Adventure Tips 82
    Packing Tips for UK Adventures 86
    Budget Advice for UK Adventures 89

CHAPTER 7 94

Shopping in the United Kingdom 94

    London's Luxury Shopping and Boutiques . 94
    Local Markets and Artisan Shops 96
    Best Places to Buy Souvenirs 98
    How to Avoid Common Scams 101
    Best Shopping Tips for the UK 104

CHAPTER 8 109

Accommodations: Where to Stay in the UK 109

    Luxury Hotels and Boutique Stays 109
    Budget-Friendly Options 111
    Unique Stays: Castles, Cottages, and More 113
    Sample Budget for Accommodations in the UK 116

        1. London's Luxury Shopping and

Boutiques 121

2. Local Markets and Artisan Shops 121

3. Best Places to Buy Souvenirs 121

CHAPTER 9 123

Transportation and Getting Around 123

Public Transportation: Trains, Buses, and More 123

Renting a Car and Driving in the UK 126

Tips for Navigating Cities and Countryside 128

Local Transit: Navigating Cities with Ease 131

Exploring Rural Areas by Local Transit 135

Travel Cards and Discount Options 136

Sample Budget for Transportation and Getting Around the UK 137

CHAPTER 10 141

Planning Your Budget: A Guide to Estimating Costs for Your UK Trip 141

Estimating Costs for Your Trip 142

Saving Money: Travel Hacks and Deals 145

Currency, Tipping, and Handling Money in the UK 147

CHAPTER 11 150

Practical Tips and Advice for Your UK Journey 150

Safety and Health Precautions 150

Etiquette and Customs 152

Language, Weather, and Time Zones 154

Staying Connected 156

Emergency Numbers and Contacts 156

    Non-Urgent Medical Assistance: NHS 111 158

    Embassies and Consulates 159

    Important Travel Insurance Contacts 161

    Local Health Services and Pharmacies .. 162

    Keeping a Personal Emergency Kit. 163

CHAPTER 11 165

Sustainable Travel in the UK 165

Eco-Friendly Travel Tips 166

Supporting Local Communities................ 168
Traveling Responsibly............................. 170
Itinerary Tips for Sustainable Travel in the UK..172

    1. Plan Around Public Transportation... 173

    2. Prioritize Longer Stays in Each Location.. 173

    3. Explore National Parks and Nature Reserves..174

    4. Visit Off-the-Beaten-Path Locations. 175

    5. Support Local Businesses and Sustainable Tours..............................176

    6. Book Accommodations in Central Locations... 176

    7. Time Your Visit to Avoid Peak Tourist Seasons............................... 177

    8. Combine Cities and Nature for a Balanced Experience........................ 178

    9. Pack Smart for the UK's Variable Weather.. 179

10. Be Flexible and Open to Spontaneous Experiences................ 179
Best Travel Apps for Exploring the UK.... 180
- 1. Citymapper.................................. 180
- 2. Trainline..181
- 3. National Trust and English Heritage Apps...181
- 4. Google Maps............................... 182
- 5. Airbnb.. 183
- 6. Skyscanner.................................. 183
- 7. Rome2Rio.................................... 184
- 8. XE Currency............................... 184
- 9. TripIt.. 185
- 10. Good Pub Guide........................ 185
- 11. UK Weather Apps (BBC Weather or Met Office).................................. 186
- 12. Green Travel Apps..................... 186

Conclusion.. 188

Leaving with Memories and New Insights.. 189

Sustainable Travel Practices for the

Future...190
Acknowledgments..**192**
Appendix..**195**
    Useful Contacts and Resources........ 195
    Maps of the UK................................ 197
    Recommended Reading and Further
    Information.. 198
    Frequently Asked Questions (FAQ) 199

Copyright © 2024 by Emily Hawthorne

All rights reserved. No part of this book may be reproduced, distributed, or transmitted in any form or by any means, including photocopying, recording, or other electronic or mechanical methods, without the prior written permission of the publisher, except in the case of brief quotations embodied in critical reviews and certain other non-commercial uses permitted by copyright law.

Introduction

Welcome to the United Kingdom

The United Kingdom is a land of diverse landscapes, rich history, and vibrant culture, offering an array of experiences that captivate travelers from around the globe. Comprising England, Scotland, Wales, and Northern Ireland, each part of the UK has its own unique charm and character. From the bustling capital of London to the tranquil beauty of the Lake District, the UK is a destination that promises both adventure and relaxation.

England is renowned for its iconic landmarks such as the Tower of London, Buckingham Palace, and the historic universities of Oxford and Cambridge. The bustling metropolis of London is a hub of culture, finance, and entertainment, offering everything from world-class museums and theaters to trendy neighborhoods and culinary delights.

Scotland enchants with its rugged highlands, ancient castles, and charming cities like Edinburgh and Glasgow. The historic and cultural richness of Scotland is showcased in its festivals, whisky trails, and picturesque landscapes, including the famous Loch Ness and the Isle of Skye.

Wales boasts stunning natural scenery, from the majestic Snowdonia National Park to the picturesque coastal towns like Tenby and Aberystwyth. Known for its vibrant cultural heritage, including the Welsh language and traditional music, Wales offers a blend of history and natural beauty.

Northern Ireland is a land of dramatic coastlines, lush green countryside, and rich history. The Giant's Causeway, a UNESCO World Heritage site, is just one of its natural wonders, while cities like Belfast and Derry offer a mix of historical and modern attractions.

Why Visit the UK in 2024-2025?

Visiting the UK in 2024-2025 presents a unique opportunity to experience a country undergoing exciting transformations and celebrations. Here's why the coming years are an ideal time to explore:

1. **Cultural Renaissance**: The UK's cultural scene is in full swing with numerous events and festivals scheduled. Edinburgh will host its renowned Festival Fringe, a celebration of arts and performance, while London's West End will feature new and acclaimed productions. The UK will also welcome international musicians and artists to various festivals throughout the year, including Glastonbury, one of the world's largest and most famous music festivals.

2. **Historical Milestones**: Several significant anniversaries and commemorations will take place in 2025. These include the 80th anniversary of the end of World War II, with events and exhibitions reflecting on this pivotal period.

Additionally, royal celebrations at historic sites like Windsor Castle will mark important milestones in the British monarchy.

3. **Sustainability Efforts**: The UK is at the forefront of sustainable tourism, with an increasing number of eco-friendly hotels, green travel initiatives, and conservation projects. The push for sustainability is evident in the efforts to reduce carbon footprints, promote local produce, and protect natural environments, allowing travelers to enjoy their visit while supporting eco-conscious practices.

4. **Modern Infrastructure**: The UK continues to invest in its infrastructure, making travel more accessible and enjoyable. High-speed rail networks, such as the HS2, are expanding, reducing travel times between major cities. Additionally, improvements in air travel and local transport services ensure that exploring the UK is more convenient than ever.

How to Use This Guide

This guide is structured to provide you with a comprehensive overview of the UK and assist you in planning a memorable trip. Here's how to navigate through the content:

Planning Your Trip: The initial sections will help you with the essentials of planning your journey. This includes advice on the best times to visit, flight options, visa requirements, and preliminary budgeting.

Exploring the Regions: Detailed chapters on each region—England, Scotland, Wales, and Northern Ireland—will offer in-depth information about key cities, towns, and attractions. You'll find recommendations for must-see landmarks, historical sites, and cultural experiences.

Local Experiences: Discover the UK's culinary scene, local traditions, and unique experiences. From traditional British fare to modern dining, from historical reenactments to local festivals, this guide covers the diverse experiences that make the UK special.

Practical Tips: Essential travel advice including transportation options, accommodation types, safety tips, and health recommendations will ensure that you are well-prepared for your trip. This section also addresses common travel concerns and provides practical solutions.

Hidden Gems: Beyond the well-trodden paths, explore off-the-beaten-track destinations and lesser-known attractions that offer unique and memorable experiences. This section highlights charming villages, scenic spots, and cultural treasures that might not be on the typical tourist radar.

With this guide in hand, you're equipped to uncover the very best of the United Kingdom, making the most of every moment of your journey. Enjoy the adventure and the wealth of experiences that await you!

CHAPTER 1

Getting To The United Kingdom

International Flights

The journey to the United Kingdom begins at one of its major international airports, each serving as a key entry point to the country. London Heathrow Airport is the largest and most prominent gateway. Located approximately 25 kilometers west of central London, it is not just a major hub for international flights but also a crucial transit point for travelers heading to other destinations in the UK and Europe. With five terminals, Heathrow offers extensive facilities, including lounges, shopping, and dining options, to ensure a comfortable start to your journey.

London Gatwick Airport, situated about 45 kilometers south of central London, is another major airport serving the capital and surrounding areas. Gatwick is known for its efficiency and range of international connections. Its two terminals are equipped with a variety of services, including shops, restaurants, and car rental facilities, catering to the needs of travelers.

For those seeking budget-friendly travel options, London Stansted Airport provides an array of low-cost and charter airlines. Located about 48 kilometers northeast of London, Stansted primarily serves as a base for budget carriers and offers a more streamlined travel experience, though it is less expansive than Heathrow or Gatwick.

In northern England, Manchester Airport is a significant hub with connections to major cities across the globe. It serves as a vital entry point for travelers exploring the northern regions of England, including Liverpool and Leeds. Manchester Airport is well-regarded for its modern facilities and passenger services, including a wide range of shopping and dining options.

Scotland's primary gateway is Edinburgh Airport, which provides both international and domestic flights. Situated a short distance from Scotland's capital city, Edinburgh Airport is known for its welcoming atmosphere and efficient services. It offers connections to various European and North American cities, making it a key entry point for visitors interested in Scotland's rich cultural and historical heritage.

Glasgow Airport, located near Scotland's largest city, is another important airport for international travel. It serves as a major gateway for travelers heading to Glasgow and the surrounding areas, with flights connecting to numerous international destinations.

For travelers heading to Northern Ireland, Belfast is served by two airports: Belfast International and George Best Belfast City Airport. Belfast International, situated about 21 kilometers west of the city center, handles a wide range of international flights. George Best Belfast City Airport, closer to the city center, primarily offers flights to and from UK and European destinations.

Entry Requirements and Visas

Understanding the entry requirements and visa regulations is crucial for a smooth travel experience. Depending on your nationality, you may be required to obtain a visa before arriving in the UK. Citizens of many countries, including the United States, Canada, Australia, and EU member states, can visit the UK for short stays of up to six months without a visa. These travelers can enter the UK for tourism, business, or family visits.

For travelers from countries outside this list, a Standard Visitor Visa may be required. This visa allows for a stay of up to six months and is applicable for purposes such as tourism, business meetings, or short-term studies. The application process generally involves providing evidence of financial means, accommodation details, and the purpose of the visit.

Starting in late 2024, the UK will implement an Electronic Travel Authorisation (ETA) system for visitors from visa-exempt countries. This electronic system is designed to pre-screen travelers before they board their flight to the UK. Applicants will need to provide personal details, travel information, and passport details to obtain the ETA, which will be electronically linked to their passport.

When traveling to the UK, be aware of customs regulations that govern the import of goods. This includes understanding restrictions on certain items, such as agricultural products and medications, as well as duty-free allowances for personal items. Familiarize yourself with the rules to avoid any issues upon arrival.

Best Times to Visit

The climate in the UK is characterized by mild temperatures and frequent rainfall, with distinct seasonal variations that can influence the best time to visit. Spring, from March to May, is a particularly delightful time to explore the UK. The weather is generally mild, and the countryside comes alive with blooming flowers and lush greenery. This season is ideal for enjoying outdoor activities, visiting gardens, and exploring historic sites with fewer crowds compared to the peak summer months.

Summer, running from June to August, offers warmer temperatures and longer daylight hours. This is the peak tourist season, with numerous festivals, outdoor events, and attractions drawing large crowds. If you plan to visit during this time, booking accommodations and tickets in advance is advisable to secure your preferred options and avoid long lines at popular attractions.

Autumn, from September to November, is characterized by cooler temperatures and vibrant fall foliage. This season offers a more relaxed travel experience, with fewer tourists and the opportunity to enjoy cultural events, harvest festivals, and scenic landscapes adorned in autumn colors.

Winter, from December to February, brings a unique charm to the UK with festive holiday decorations, Christmas markets, and seasonal events. While temperatures can be cold and wet, the winter months offer a cozy atmosphere and lower travel costs. If you enjoy winter activities, such as ice skating and festive markets, this is an excellent time to visit.

Travel Insurance

Travel insurance is an essential aspect of trip planning, offering protection against a range of potential issues. It is advisable to select a comprehensive travel insurance policy that covers medical emergencies, trip cancellations, lost luggage, and other unforeseen events. Ensure that the policy includes coverage for any specific activities you plan to undertake, such as adventure sports or extended stays.

Travel insurance provides peace of mind, allowing you to focus on enjoying your trip rather than worrying about potential disruptions. Before purchasing insurance, carefully review the policy details and coverage options to ensure they meet your needs.

Health and Safety

The UK boasts a well-developed healthcare system, ensuring that medical services are readily available. For travelers from EU countries, the European Health Insurance Card (EHIC) or the Global Health Insurance Card (GHIC) provides access to necessary medical treatment during your stay. Travelers from other countries should ensure they have adequate travel insurance coverage that includes health care expenses.

In terms of safety, the UK is generally a secure destination for tourists. However, it is always prudent to exercise common-sense precautions. Keep your belongings secure, stay aware of your surroundings, and follow local laws and regulations. The UK has a relatively low crime rate, but being cautious and vigilant will contribute to a safer travel experience.

CHAPTER 2

Exploring the Regions of the UK

England: History, Culture, and Vibrant Cities

England, with its blend of historic charm and modern vibrancy, offers a wealth of experiences for travelers. London, the nation's capital, stands as a cultural and historical epicenter. Beyond the famous landmarks like the Houses of Parliament and Buckingham Palace, London boasts a dynamic arts scene, with renowned institutions such as the Tate Modern and the National Gallery. The city's diverse neighborhoods, from the trendy streets of Shoreditch to the historic allure of Covent Garden, offer a rich tapestry of experiences. Explore the historic markets of Borough and Portobello Road, or take a leisurely stroll along the South Bank to enjoy views of the Thames and the London Eye.

Venturing beyond London, the historic university cities of Oxford and Cambridge offer a glimpse into England's academic heritage. Oxford, with its ancient colleges and beautiful libraries, is a city steeped in intellectual history. Cambridge, known for its picturesque colleges and the serene River Cam, is equally captivating. Both cities provide a charming blend of historic architecture and vibrant student life.

The vibrant northern cities of Manchester and Liverpool are cultural powerhouses in their own right. Manchester, often regarded as the "capital of the North," is celebrated for its music scene, including iconic venues such as the Manchester Arena and the Royal Exchange Theatre. Liverpool, famous for its maritime heritage and as the birthplace of The Beatles, boasts attractions like The Beatles Story museum and the Albert Dock, a UNESCO World Heritage site.

England's countryside is a treasure trove of natural beauty and historic charm. The Cotswolds, with its quintessentially English villages and rolling hills, offer a tranquil retreat from the city. Explore the charming towns of Bourton-on-the-Water and Chipping Campden, known for their thatched-roof cottages and scenic walking trails. The Lake District, a UNESCO World Heritage site, is a haven for outdoor enthusiasts, with its stunning lakes, forested hills, and scenic hiking routes. Be sure to visit Windermere and Keswick, both popular starting points for exploring the area's natural splendor.

Bath, with its Georgian architecture and Roman baths, provides a fascinating blend of history and elegance. The city's Bath Abbey and the Royal Crescent are architectural highlights, while the thermal spa offers a unique opportunity to relax in naturally heated waters.

Scotland: Highlands, Castles, and Traditions

Scotland is a land of dramatic landscapes, rich heritage, and vibrant cultural traditions. Edinburgh, Scotland's capital, is a city where history and culture intersect magnificently. Edinburgh Castle dominates the skyline, offering panoramic views of the city and insight into Scotland's storied past. The Royal Mile, stretching from the castle to the Palace of Holyroodhouse, is lined with historic sites, shops, and traditional Scottish pubs. The Edinburgh Festival Fringe, held every August, transforms the city into a bustling hub of performance arts, showcasing a diverse array of shows and talent.

Glasgow, Scotland's largest city, presents a dynamic cultural scene with a mix of historic and modern influences. The city's architectural marvels, such as the Glasgow School of Art designed by Charles Rennie Mackintosh, are complemented by vibrant museums like the Kelvingrove Art Gallery and Museum. Glasgow's West End, with its lively nightlife, eclectic restaurants, and independent shops, offers a contrasting experience to the city's more traditional areas.

The Scottish Highlands, with their rugged beauty and remote charm, are a must-see for nature lovers and history enthusiasts alike. The region is home to iconic landmarks such as Loch Ness, famed for its legendary monster and picturesque setting. The surrounding area, including the scenic shores of Loch Lomond and the Trossachs National Park, offers ample opportunities for outdoor adventures. The Isle of Skye, known for its dramatic landscapes, including the Quiraing and the Old Man of Storr, is a haven for hikers and photographers seeking stunning vistas.

Scotland's castles, including Eilean Donan Castle, perched on a small island in Loch Duich, and Urquhart Castle, overlooking Loch Ness, provide a glimpse into the country's medieval past. Each castle is steeped in history and surrounded by breathtaking landscapes.

Wales: Natural Beauty and Coastal Adventures

Wales is renowned for its striking landscapes and deep cultural roots. Cardiff, the capital city, is a blend of modernity and tradition. Cardiff Castle, located in the heart of the city, offers a journey through Welsh history with its medieval and Victorian architecture. The National Museum Cardiff, with its diverse collections of art and natural history, provides insight into Welsh heritage and culture.

North Wales is a region of rugged beauty and outdoor adventure. Snowdonia National Park, with its dramatic mountain scenery, is a paradise for hikers and climbers. The ascent of Mount Snowdon, the highest peak in Wales, offers spectacular views over the surrounding landscape. The nearby town of Betws-y-Coed, nestled in the heart of Snowdonia, serves as a gateway to outdoor activities and scenic exploration.

The coastal towns of Conwy and Llandudno offer charming seaside experiences. Conwy, with its well-preserved medieval walls and Conwy Castle, provides a glimpse into Wales's historical fortifications. Llandudno, with its Victorian architecture and picturesque pier, offers a classic British seaside experience.

South Wales is equally captivating, with the Gower Peninsula and Pembrokeshire Coast offering dramatic coastal scenery and opportunities for outdoor activities. The Gower Peninsula, known for its stunning beaches and coastal walks, was the first area in the UK to be designated an Area of Outstanding Natural Beauty. Pembrokeshire Coast National Park, with its rugged cliffs and beautiful beaches, is ideal for coastal walks and wildlife watching. The Brecon Beacons National Park, with its rolling hills, waterfalls, and charming villages, provides a serene escape into nature.

Wales is also celebrated for its strong cultural identity. The Welsh language, still widely spoken, and traditional music are integral to Welsh culture, celebrated in various festivals and events throughout the year. The National Eisteddfod, a major cultural festival, showcases Welsh music, literature, and performance.

Northern Ireland: Ancient History and Modern Culture

Northern Ireland is a region rich in history and modern cultural vibrancy. Belfast, the capital, is a city of transformation and heritage. The Titanic Belfast museum, located on the site where the RMS Titanic was built, offers an immersive experience into the ship's history and the city's maritime heritage. The Cathedral Quarter, known for its lively arts scene and historic pubs, is a focal point for nightlife and cultural events.

Derry, or Londonderry, is a city with a well-preserved history and a vibrant contemporary culture. The city walls, which date back to the early 17th century, offer a historic walk around the city center, providing views of the modern and historic cityscape. Derry's cultural scene is enriched by festivals and events that celebrate its history and diversity.

Northern Ireland's natural beauty is striking, with landmarks such as the Giant's Causeway—a UNESCO World Heritage site renowned for its unique basalt columns formed by volcanic activity—drawing visitors from around the world. The Causeway Coastal Route, which stretches from Belfast to Derry, offers a spectacular drive with breathtaking coastal views, charming towns, and historic sites.

The Mourne Mountains, located in County Down, provide opportunities for hiking and exploring rugged landscapes. The area is known for its natural beauty and is a popular destination for outdoor enthusiasts seeking to experience the serene beauty of Northern Ireland's countryside.

CHAPTER 3

Top Attractions and Must-See Sights

London's Icons

The Houses of Parliament and Big Ben: The Houses of Parliament, also known as the Palace of Westminster, are not just political headquarters but architectural marvels. The building's intricate Gothic Revival design, featuring towers, spires, and elaborate stonework, reflects centuries of British history and politics. The Elizabeth Tower, commonly called Big Ben, remains a quintessential symbol of London, and the ongoing restoration work is aimed at preserving its iconic status. Visitors can admire its external beauty and explore the nearby Westminster Abbey, another historical and architectural gem.

The British Museum: This cultural institution is one of the world's oldest and most comprehensive museums. Its diverse collection spans from ancient Egypt to modern cultures, with highlights such as the Rosetta Stone, which unlocked the secrets of Egyptian hieroglyphs, and the Elgin Marbles from the Parthenon. The museum's Great Court, designed by architect Norman Foster, is an architectural wonder in itself, featuring a stunning glass roof and providing a central space for visitors to gather and explore.

Buckingham Palace: Buckingham Palace is more than just a royal residence; it's a symbol of the British monarchy and national heritage. The State Rooms, open to the public during the summer, offer a glimpse into the opulent world of royal ceremonies and state functions. The Changing of the Guard ceremony, a colorful spectacle of precision and pageantry, occurs regularly and draws crowds eager to witness this British tradition.

The Tower of London: With its centuries of history, the Tower of London is a must-visit for those interested in

British royalty and intrigue. Beyond the Crown Jewels, the White Tower houses medieval armor and the famous Beefeaters, who serve as both ceremonial guards and guides. The tower's history includes roles as a royal palace, prison, and mint, making it a fascinating destination for history enthusiasts.

The London Eye: This modern marvel provides a unique vantage point over London. From its spacious capsules, visitors can enjoy 360-degree views of the city, encompassing landmarks like St. Paul's Cathedral, the Shard, and the River Thames. The London Eye's location on the South Bank places it near other attractions such as the Tate Modern and the London Dungeon, creating a hub of entertainment and culture.

Historic Sites Across England

Stonehenge: This prehistoric monument is one of the most famous archaeological sites in the world. The site's massive stone circle, constructed between 3000 and 2000 BC, remains a subject of fascination and speculation. The visitor center offers detailed exhibits about the construction methods and the possible astronomical and ceremonial purposes of Stonehenge, enhancing the visitor experience.

Bath: The city of Bath, renowned for its Roman Baths and Georgian architecture, provides a blend of historical and architectural splendor. The Roman Baths complex includes the Great Bath, the Roman Temple, and the Bath House, all showcasing the city's Roman heritage. The Georgian architecture of the Royal Crescent and the Circus offers a glimpse into the elegance of 18th-century Bath, with its sweeping crescents and classical facades.

Hadrian's Wall: Stretching across northern England, Hadrian's Wall is a testament to Roman engineering and military history. The wall, built by Emperor Hadrian to mark the northern boundary of the Roman Empire, offers a scenic walking route through Northumberland and Cumbria. Key sites along the wall, such as Housesteads Fort and Vindolanda, provide insight into Roman life and fortifications.

Warwick Castle: This medieval fortress, originally built by William the Conqueror, is a well-preserved example of medieval military architecture. The castle's Great Hall, dungeons, and towers offer a glimpse into medieval life, while interactive exhibits and historical reenactments bring its history to life. The castle's extensive grounds include beautiful gardens and scenic views of the surrounding Warwickshire countryside.

Scotland's Historic and Natural Wonders

Edinburgh Castle: Dominating the skyline of Edinburgh, this historic fortress is a focal point of Scotland's capital. The castle's historical significance is evident in its role as a royal residence and military stronghold. Highlights include the Crown Jewels of Scotland, the Stone of Destiny, and the One O'Clock Gun. The castle's strategic location on Castle Rock provides panoramic views over Edinburgh and the surrounding area.

The Royal Mile: This historic thoroughfare in Edinburgh connects Edinburgh Castle to the Palace of Holyroodhouse. The Royal Mile is lined with historic buildings, including St Giles' Cathedral and the Real Mary King's Close, an underground network of preserved 17th-century streets. The street's vibrant atmosphere, with its shops, cafes, and traditional Scottish pubs, offers a lively and immersive experience of Edinburgh's history and culture.

Loch Ness: Famous for its legendary monster, Loch Ness is a stunning natural attraction in the Scottish Highlands. The loch's serene waters and surrounding landscapes offer opportunities for boat tours and scenic exploration. The Loch Ness Centre and Exhibition provides information about the loch's history, the monster legend, and the region's natural beauty.

Eilean Donan Castle: This picturesque castle, situated on an island at the confluence of three lochs, is one of Scotland's most iconic landmarks. Eilean Donan Castle's romantic setting and well-preserved interiors make it a popular destination for visitors exploring the Highlands. The castle's history dates back to the 13th century, and its scenic location provides a stunning backdrop for photographs.

The Isle of Skye: Known for its dramatic landscapes and natural beauty, the Isle of Skye offers a range of outdoor activities and scenic vistas. The Quiraing, with its surreal rock formations and rolling hills, and the Old Man of Storr, a striking rock spire, are highlights of the island's rugged terrain. Skye's villages, such as Portree, provide charming accommodations and local cuisine, making it a perfect base for exploring the island.

Wales' Natural and Historical Highlights

Cardiff Castle: Located in the heart of Cardiff, this historic fortress combines Roman, medieval, and Victorian architecture. The castle's interior includes the lavishly decorated apartments and the medieval remains of the Roman fort. The castle's central location and historical significance make it a focal point of Cardiff's cultural and historical heritage.

Snowdonia National Park: This national park is renowned for its stunning mountain scenery and outdoor activities. Mount Snowdon, the highest peak in Wales, offers hiking trails and breathtaking views. The park also features picturesque lakes, such as Llyn Padarn, and charming villages like Beddgelert, known for its beautiful scenery and local legends.

Conwy Castle: A well-preserved medieval fortress in North Wales, Conwy Castle is a UNESCO World Heritage site. Built by Edward I, the castle's imposing walls and towers provide insight into medieval military architecture. The town of Conwy, with its historic walls and charming streets, complements the castle's historical significance.

The Brecon Beacons National Park: This national park is known for its scenic landscapes and outdoor activities.

Pen y Fan, the highest peak in the park, offers excellent hiking opportunities with panoramic views. The park also features waterfalls such as Sgwd yr Eira, where visitors can walk behind the falls and enjoy the natural beauty of the region.

Northern Ireland's Unique Attractions

Titanic Belfast: Located in the Titanic Quarter of Belfast, this museum offers an immersive experience into the history of the RMS Titanic. The museum's interactive exhibits cover the ship's construction, launch, and tragic sinking. The museum's striking architecture and detailed exhibits make it a key destination for visitors interested in maritime history.

The Giant's Causeway: This natural wonder features thousands of interlocking basalt columns formed by volcanic activity. The Giant's Causeway is a UNESCO

World Heritage site known for its unique geological formations and stunning coastal scenery. Visitors can explore the formations and enjoy guided tours that explain the site's geological and mythological significance.

Derry/Londonderry: Known for its well-preserved city walls and historic buildings, Derry/Londonderry offers a rich cultural and historical experience. The city's walls, built in the early 17th century, provide a scenic walk with views over the city and its surroundings. The city also hosts various festivals and events that celebrate its heritage and vibrant cultural scene.

The Mourne Mountains: This mountain range in County Down is known for its rugged beauty and outdoor adventures. The Mourne Mountains feature peaks such as Slieve Donard, the highest mountain in Northern Ireland. The area's stunning landscapes and serene environment make it a popular destination for hiking and nature enthusiasts.

CHAPTER 4

Cultural Experiences Across the UK

The British Museum and Other World-Class Museums

The British Museum: Located in Bloomsbury, London, the British Museum is an architectural and cultural landmark, renowned for its vast and diverse collections. The museum's history stretches back to 1753, when it was founded based on the collection of Sir Hans Sloane. Its exhibits cover every continent and era, including artifacts from ancient Mesopotamia, such as the Ishtar Gate, and the Assyrian Lion Hunt reliefs. The museum's galleries offer insights into the evolution of human societies, art, and culture. The museum's ongoing conservation efforts ensure that these priceless items are preserved for future generations, while its educational programs and research contribute to global knowledge.

The Tate Modern: This museum's transformation from a power station into a contemporary art museum is a testament to innovative reuse of historic buildings. The Tate Modern's collection includes works from Picasso's Blue Period to Damien Hirst's provocative installations. The Turbine Hall, a vast space within the museum, is known for hosting large-scale installations by leading contemporary artists, such as Anish Kapoor and Olafur Eliasson. The museum also features a dedicated space for temporary exhibitions, allowing visitors to experience cutting-edge art trends.

The Natural History Museum: This museum's rich collection includes over 80 million specimens, with highlights such as the life-sized model of a blue whale and the impressive dinosaur gallery, featuring the towering Diplodocus skeleton. The museum's Earth Hall, with its central asteroid impact crater, explores the planet's formation and natural processes. The museum's scientific research and conservation initiatives play a crucial role in understanding and preserving biodiversity.

The Victoria and Albert Museum: Known as the V&A, this museum is dedicated to decorative arts and design, with over 2.27 million objects spanning 5,000 years. Highlights include the stunning Raphael Cartoons, the exquisite jewelry collection, and the elaborate textiles gallery. The museum's Theatre and Performance galleries showcase theatrical costumes, props, and set designs, offering a glimpse into the history of performance arts. The V&A's Design Museum, located in the same building, focuses on industrial design and innovation.

The Science Museum: This museum is a treasure trove of scientific knowledge and innovation. The Space Gallery features artifacts from the Apollo missions, including the command module. The Information Age gallery traces the evolution of communication technology from the telegraph to the internet. The museum's interactive exhibits, such as the Wonderlab, engage visitors of all ages with hands-on experiments and demonstrations.

Music, Festivals, and Events

London's Music Scene: London is a global hub for music, offering a wide range of genres and live performances. The Royal Albert Hall, an iconic venue in Kensington, hosts classical concerts, rock performances, and more. The O2 Arena, located in Greenwich, is a major venue for international pop and rock stars. For a more intimate experience, venues like Ronnie Scott's Jazz Club in Soho provide live jazz performances in a historic setting.

Edinburgh Festival Fringe: Held annually in August, the Edinburgh Festival Fringe is the world's largest arts festival. It features thousands of performances across genres including theatre, comedy, dance, and music. The festival transforms the city into a vibrant cultural hub, with street performances, pop-up venues, and an eclectic mix of shows. The Fringe is renowned for showcasing emerging talent and innovative performances.

Glastonbury Festival: One of the UK's most famous music festivals, Glastonbury takes place in Somerset and attracts music lovers from around the world. The festival features a diverse lineup of artists, ranging from legendary bands to contemporary stars, and includes a wide range of performances beyond music, such as dance, theater, and circus acts. The event is known for its iconic Pyramid Stage and its commitment to sustainability and social issues.

The Proms: Held annually at the Royal Albert Hall, The Proms is an eight-week summer season of classical concerts. The festival, officially known as the BBC Proms, offers a wide range of classical music performances, including orchestral works, choral music, and solo recitals. The Proms are known for their accessibility, with many concerts featuring affordable or standing-room tickets, and for the famous Last Night of the Proms, which concludes with a celebratory and patriotic concert.

Notting Hill Carnival: Taking place in August, the Notting Hill Carnival is Europe's largest street festival, celebrating Caribbean culture with vibrant parades, music, and dance. The carnival features colorful costumes, reggae and calypso music, and a variety of food stalls offering Caribbean cuisine. The event draws visitors from across London and beyond, showcasing the city's multicultural heritage and lively spirit.

Theatre and the Arts in London's West End

West End Theatre District: London's West End is synonymous with world-class theatre and musicals. The district's theaters host a variety of performances, from long-running shows like "The Phantom of the Opera" and "Les Misérables" to new productions and experimental works. The West End's historic theaters, such as the Adelphi Theatre and the Old Vic, offer an opulent setting for enjoying some of the best theatre performances in the world.

The Royal Opera House: Located in Covent Garden, the Royal Opera House is a premier venue for opera and ballet. The house is home to The Royal Opera and The Royal Ballet, and its productions are renowned for their artistic excellence and grand staging. The opera house's stunning architecture and interiors provide a fitting backdrop for performances ranging from classic operas to contemporary works.

Shakespeare's Globe Theatre: A replica of the original Elizabethan theatre where Shakespeare's plays were performed, Shakespeare's Globe offers an immersive experience into the world of 16th-century theatre. The open-air theatre provides performances of Shakespeare's plays in a historically accurate setting, with actors performing in period costumes and using traditional staging techniques.

National Theatre: Situated on the South Bank of the Thames, the National Theatre is a major producing house that presents a diverse range of productions, from classic plays to contemporary works. The theatre's repertoire includes innovative adaptations, new writing, and high-profile productions featuring prominent actors and directors. The National Theatre also offers educational programs and workshops for those interested in theatre and drama.

The Barbican Centre: As one of London's largest and most versatile arts venues, the Barbican Centre hosts a wide range of cultural events, including concerts, theatre performances, film screenings, and art exhibitions. The centre's Brutalist architecture and extensive facilities make it a key destination for exploring contemporary and classical art forms.

Music Festivals Across the UK

The UK is renowned for its vibrant and diverse music festival scene, offering something for every taste, from intimate gatherings to massive events that attract thousands. Here's an expanded look at some of the most notable music festivals across the country:

Glastonbury Festival

Overview: Glastonbury Festival, held annually in Somerset, is one of the largest and most famous music festivals in the world. Founded in 1970 by Michael Eavis, it has grown from a small, free event to a multi-day festival featuring a diverse lineup of international and local artists.

Features: Glastonbury's iconic Pyramid Stage is a centerpiece of the festival, hosting headline acts from various genres, including rock, pop, and hip-hop. Beyond the Pyramid Stage, the festival offers a range of stages and areas dedicated to different musical styles, such as the John Peel Stage for emerging talent and the West

Holts Stage for world music. The festival is also known for its emphasis on arts and sustainability, with areas dedicated to theatre, circus performances, and environmental initiatives.

Highlights: Glastonbury is celebrated for its eclectic lineup, which has included legendary performances by artists such as David Bowie, Beyoncé, and Paul McCartney. The festival's atmosphere is vibrant and communal, with attendees enjoying not only the music but also the arts, food, and workshops.

Reading and Leeds Festivals

Overview: Reading and Leeds Festivals are twin music festivals that take place simultaneously over the August Bank Holiday weekend. Established in the 1960s, these festivals are among the oldest and most significant in the UK, attracting a diverse range of music fans.

Features: The festivals feature multiple stages showcasing a mix of rock, alternative, and indie music. The Reading Festival, held at Richfield Avenue in

Reading, and the Leeds Festival, at Bramham Park in Leeds, share lineups, but each festival offers its own unique atmosphere. The stages include the Main Stage for major headliners, the Radio 1 Stage for up-and-coming acts, and the Lock-Up Stage for punk and metal.

Highlights: Known for their high-energy performances and historic lineups, Reading and Leeds Festivals have hosted iconic acts like Nirvana, Arctic Monkeys, and The Killers. The festivals are popular with younger audiences and offer a range of additional activities, including comedy and alternative entertainment.

The Isle of Wight Festival

Overview: The Isle of Wight Festival is a historic event that first took place in 1968 and has since become a major annual music festival. Held on the Isle of Wight, this festival is known for its scenic location and diverse lineup.

Features: The festival includes several stages, with the Main Stage featuring top international and UK acts. The site is set against the backdrop of the island's natural beauty, providing a picturesque setting for performances. The festival also offers family-friendly activities and a range of food and craft stalls.

Highlights: The Isle of Wight Festival is known for its storied past, including legendary performances by Jimi Hendrix and The Who. Recent lineups have featured artists like David Bowie, The Stone Roses, and Fleetwood Mac. The festival combines a rich musical heritage with modern performances, appealing to a broad audience.

Creamfields

Overview: Creamfields is one of the UK's largest electronic music festivals, focusing on dance, house, and techno. Held annually in Cheshire, it was first organized by the Cream nightclub in Liverpool in 1998 and has since become a major event in the electronic music calendar.

Features: The festival features multiple stages dedicated to various sub-genres of electronic music, including house, techno, and drum and bass. It attracts some of the biggest names in electronic music, as well as emerging artists. Creamfields is renowned for its impressive stage designs, light shows, and immersive festival experience.

Highlights: Creamfields has hosted performances by leading electronic artists such as Calvin Harris, David Guetta, and Deadmau5. The festival is known for its high-energy atmosphere and cutting-edge production values, making it a must-attend event for electronic music fans.

Glastonbury Festival of Contemporary Performing Arts

Overview: Often referred to simply as Glastonbury, this festival is a comprehensive celebration of contemporary performing arts, with music being a central component. Held at Worthy Farm in Somerset, it spans several days and features a broad range of artistic performances.

Features: In addition to its extensive music lineup, Glastonbury offers a rich array of performance arts, including theatre, dance, and spoken word. The festival is known for its diverse range of stages and areas, each offering a different type of entertainment, from mainstream acts to experimental performances. The festival's environmental and social activism is a key aspect, with various initiatives aimed at promoting sustainability and community engagement.

Highlights: Glastonbury is renowned for its legendary performances and cultural significance, with past headliners including The Rolling Stones, Adele, and Radiohead. The festival's commitment to arts and social causes, combined with its unique atmosphere, makes it a landmark event in the UK festival scene.

The Secret Garden Party

Overview: The Secret Garden Party is an independent festival held in Cambridgeshire, known for its intimate and eclectic atmosphere. Founded in 2004, it offers a unique and immersive experience that combines music with art and interactive experiences.

Features: The festival features a diverse lineup of music across multiple stages, including electronic, indie, and folk. It also offers a range of art installations, workshops, and interactive performances. The Secret Garden Party's emphasis on creativity and community creates a distinctive festival experience that encourages exploration and participation.

Highlights: The Secret Garden Party is celebrated for its whimsical and artistic environment, with themes and decorations that transform the festival site into a magical landscape. Past performers have included Florence + the Machine, Metronomy, and Hot Chip. The festival's focus on creativity and innovation sets it apart from more mainstream events.

South West Four

Overview: South West Four is a prominent electronic music festival held in Clapham Common, London.

Established in 2004, it focuses on house, techno, and dance music and is known for its high-profile lineups and vibrant city location.

Features: The festival features several stages dedicated to electronic music, with performances by leading DJs and producers. South West Four is known for its urban setting, offering a festival experience in the heart of London. The event attracts a diverse audience of electronic music enthusiasts and provides an exciting alternative to rural festival settings.

Highlights: South West Four has hosted renowned artists such as Calvin Harris, Tiësto, and Carl Cox. The festival's city location and impressive lineup make it a popular choice for festival-goers who want to experience top electronic music in an urban environment.

The Great Escape

Overview: The Great Escape is an annual festival held in Brighton, focusing on new and emerging music talent.

Established in 2006, it has become a key event for discovering the next generation of artists.

Features: The festival features hundreds of performances across various venues in Brighton, showcasing a wide range of genres including indie, rock, and electronic music. The Great Escape is known for its industry presence, with numerous music professionals attending to scout new talent and network.

Highlights: The Great Escape has featured breakthrough artists such as Florence + the Machine, Hozier, and Rag'n'Bone Man. The festival's focus on emerging talent and its vibrant city setting make it a crucial event for music discovery and industry networking.

CHAPTER 5

Culinary Journey: Exploring British Food and Drink

Traditional British Cuisine

Traditional British cuisine is often characterized by hearty, comforting dishes that reflect the country's agricultural heritage and regional variations. Known for its simple yet satisfying flavors, British food has evolved over time, incorporating influences from around the world while maintaining its distinctive character.

One of the most iconic British dishes is fish and chips, consisting of battered and deep-fried fish, usually cod or haddock, served with thick-cut fries. Traditionally accompanied by mushy peas and tartar sauce, this dish is a staple of British cuisine and can be found in both dedicated fish and chip shops and pubs.

The Sunday roast is a beloved British tradition, typically consisting of roasted meat, such as beef, lamb, or chicken, served with roast potatoes, vegetables, Yorkshire pudding, and gravy. This meal is a focal point of family gatherings and is often enjoyed with a variety of side dishes, including stuffing and seasonal vegetables.

Shepherd's pie is a comforting dish made from minced lamb or beef, vegetables, and gravy, topped with a layer of creamy mashed potatoes. It is a hearty and warming meal, perfect for colder months. Variations include cottage pie, which uses beef instead of lamb.

Bangers and mash is a classic dish featuring sausages, often referred to as "bangers," served with mashed potatoes and often accompanied by onion gravy. It's a simple yet flavorful meal, highlighting the British love for sausages and potatoes.

Black pudding, a type of blood sausage made from pig's blood, fat, and grain, is a traditional component of the full English breakfast. It has a rich, savory flavor and is enjoyed across the UK, often served sliced and fried.

Afternoon Tea and British Pubs

Afternoon tea is a quintessential British tradition that dates back to the early 19th century. Originating as a light meal to bridge the gap between lunch and dinner, it has evolved into a more elaborate affair, often enjoyed in a leisurely setting.

Traditional afternoon tea typically includes a selection of finger sandwiches, such as cucumber, smoked salmon, and egg mayonnaise, scones served with clotted cream and jam, and an assortment of pastries and cakes. Tea is served in a pot, often accompanied by milk and sugar. Many of the UK's historic hotels and tea rooms offer afternoon tea experiences, ranging from classic settings like The Ritz in London to charming local tea rooms.

These establishments provide a range of options, from traditional to modern takes on the afternoon tea concept.

British pubs, or public houses, are central to British social life and offer a welcoming environment for enjoying drinks, food, and conversation. Many pubs serve traditional pub fare, including dishes like ploughman's lunch, which features bread, cheese, pickles, and ham, steak and ale pie, and various types of curry. Pubs often provide a relaxed atmosphere for enjoying hearty meals and local beers.

British pubs are renowned for their selection of beers and ales, including traditional cask ales, lagers, and craft beers. Pubs often feature local brews and offer a range of options to suit different tastes. The pub's role as a community hub is reflected in its emphasis on local produce and friendly service.

Local Delicacies from Each Region

England

In England, Cornish pasties are a savory pastry filled with meat, potatoes, onions, and turnips. Originating from Cornwall, these handheld pies were traditionally enjoyed by miners and remain a beloved regional specialty. Yorkshire pudding, a classic accompaniment to the Sunday roast, is a savory pastry made from batter and often served alongside roast beef and gravy. Known for its light, airy texture and crispy edges, Yorkshire pudding is a staple of British roast dinners. Cumberland sausage, hailing from Cumbria, is a distinctive coiled sausage seasoned with black pepper and other spices. It is often enjoyed grilled or as part of a traditional British breakfast.

Scotland

Scotland's national dish, haggis, is a savory pudding made from sheep's heart, liver, and lungs, mixed with oatmeal, onions, and spices. Traditionally served with neeps (turnips) and tatties (potatoes), it is a centerpiece of Burns Night celebrations. Scottish salmon, renowned for its quality, is often enjoyed smoked or fresh. Scotland's cold, clear waters provide an ideal environment for salmon farming, making it a key ingredient in Scottish cuisine. Shortbread, a buttery, crumbly biscuit, is a traditional Scottish treat enjoyed with tea. Made from simple ingredients—butter, sugar, and flour—shortbread comes in various shapes, including rounds and fingers.

Wales

In Wales, Welsh cawl is a traditional stew made with lamb or beef, leeks, potatoes, and other vegetables. Cawl is a hearty, warming dish that has been enjoyed in Wales for centuries. Laverbread, made from seaweed known as laver, is a Welsh delicacy often served with bacon, eggs, and cockles. It has a distinctive taste and is a rich source of nutrients. Bara brith, a Welsh tea bread made with dried fruits, spices, and tea, is typically enjoyed sliced and buttered and is a popular treat for afternoon tea.

Northern Ireland

Northern Ireland's Ulster fry is a traditional breakfast featuring a variety of items, including fried eggs, bacon, sausages, black pudding, white pudding, baked beans, tomatoes, and potato farls. It is a hearty and filling meal, often enjoyed as a substantial start to the day. Irish soda bread, made using baking soda as a leavening agent instead of yeast, is a staple in Northern Irish households. It can be enjoyed plain or with added ingredients like raisins or caraway seeds. The Derry Girls' Special, named after the popular TV show, includes dishes like beef and Guinness stew and potato soup, reflecting the hearty and comforting nature of Northern Irish cuisine.

Local Restaurant Tips

London: For a traditional British dining experience in London, visit **Rules** in Covent Garden, renowned for its classic British fare and historic ambiance. If you're looking for a quintessential afternoon tea experience, **The Ritz** offers an opulent setting with exceptional service. For more casual dining, **Dishoom** provides a unique fusion of British and Indian flavors in a charming setting reminiscent of a Bombay café.

Edinburgh: In Edinburgh, **The Witchery by the Castle** offers a luxurious dining experience with Scottish specialties in a historic and atmospheric setting. For an authentic taste of Scotland, **The Kitchin** provides a modern take on Scottish cuisine, with an emphasis on local and seasonal ingredients. For a more casual meal, **Oink** is famous for its delicious roast pork sandwiches, a local favorite.

Cardiff: In Cardiff, **The Potted Pig** offers a contemporary British menu in a former bank vault, known for its inventive use of local ingredients. For a traditional Welsh experience, **The Clink** is located within Cardiff Prison and serves excellent Welsh cuisine while supporting a good cause. **Chapter Arts Centre** also hosts a café with a focus on locally sourced ingredients and creative dishes.

Belfast: **The Merchant Hotel** offers a luxurious afternoon tea experience with a selection of finely crafted sandwiches, scones, and pastries. For traditional Northern Irish dishes, **The Crown Liquor Saloon** provides a historic pub setting with hearty meals and a wide range of local ales. For contemporary dining, **Eipic** offers a Michelin-starred experience with a focus on modern Irish cuisine and innovative flavors.

Local Restaurant Insights

London

Rules: Established in 1798, Rules is London's oldest restaurant, located in Covent Garden. It is renowned for its classic British cuisine, including dishes like roast game, pies, and traditional puddings. The restaurant's rich history and elegant decor make it a unique dining experience that celebrates British culinary traditions.

The Ritz: For a truly luxurious afternoon tea, The Ritz in Piccadilly is unparalleled. The opulent surroundings and impeccable service enhance the experience, which includes a selection of finely crafted sandwiches, scones with clotted cream and jam, and an array of pastries. The Ritz is a quintessential choice for a memorable afternoon tea in London.

Dishoom: Inspired by the old Irani cafés of Bombay, Dishoom offers a delightful fusion of British and Indian flavors. With its charming decor and vibrant atmosphere, Dishoom is a popular spot for breakfast, lunch, and dinner. The menu features a range of dishes from spicy street food to flavorful curries, making it a must-visit for a taste of India in London.

Sketch: Known for its quirky decor and innovative cuisine, Sketch offers a unique dining experience in Mayfair. The restaurant's Afternoon Tea is particularly famous, presented in a whimsical setting with imaginative pastries and a wide selection of teas. Sketch combines creativity with culinary excellence, making it a standout dining destination.

Edinburgh

The Witchery by the Castle: This restaurant offers a luxurious dining experience in a historic building near Edinburgh Castle. The Witchery serves classic Scottish dishes with a touch of elegance, such as haggis, venison, and an extensive selection of whiskies. The atmospheric setting adds to the charm of the dining experience.

The Kitchin: Run by Michelin-starred chef Tom Kitchin, this restaurant focuses on modern Scottish cuisine with a commitment to seasonal and local ingredients. The menu changes frequently to reflect the best of what's available, and the emphasis is on "From Nature to Plate," showcasing the finest Scottish produce in innovative ways.

Oink: For a more casual but equally delicious experience, Oink is renowned for its succulent roast pork sandwiches. Located on Victoria Street, this eatery serves flavorful, slow-roasted pork in a variety of sandwiches, making it a popular spot for a quick and satisfying meal.

Number One at The Balmoral: Situated in The Balmoral Hotel, this Michelin-starred restaurant offers a refined dining experience with a focus on Scottish ingredients. The menu features dishes such as Scottish lobster and venison, and the elegant setting provides a perfect backdrop for a special meal.

Cardiff

The Potted Pig: Housed in a former bank vault, The Potted Pig offers a contemporary British menu with a focus on locally sourced ingredients. Known for its inventive dishes and relaxed atmosphere, this restaurant is a favorite among locals and visitors alike. Highlights include slow-cooked pork belly and homemade charcuterie.

The Clink: Located within Cardiff Prison, The Clink provides an extraordinary dining experience where all profits support a charity that trains prisoners in hospitality. The menu features traditional Welsh dishes made with high-quality ingredients, and the unique setting adds an extra layer of interest to the dining experience.

Chapter Arts Centre Café: For a more casual meal, the Chapter Arts Centre Café offers a menu that emphasizes local produce and creative dishes. The café is part of a cultural hub, making it a great spot for a relaxed lunch or coffee while enjoying the vibrant arts scene in Cardiff.

The Welsh Pantry: This restaurant focuses on showcasing the best of Welsh cuisine with a modern twist. Located in the heart of Cardiff, The Welsh Pantry offers dishes like Welsh lamb and cawl, as well as a selection of local cheeses and desserts. The emphasis is on fresh, seasonal ingredients and traditional Welsh flavors.

Belfast

The Merchant Hotel: Known for its luxurious afternoon tea, The Merchant Hotel offers a refined experience with a selection of elegant sandwiches, scones with clotted cream and jam, and an array of pastries. The opulent surroundings and attentive service make it an ideal place for a special occasion or a relaxing afternoon treat.

The Crown Liquor Saloon: A historic pub with stunning Victorian decor, The Crown Liquor Saloon offers a range of traditional Northern Irish dishes and an extensive selection of local ales. The pub's unique ambiance and hearty meals make it a must-visit for a taste of Belfast's pub culture.

Eipic: This Michelin-starred restaurant offers a modern take on Irish cuisine, with a focus on seasonal ingredients and creative presentations. Eipic's menu features dishes like Irish beef and seafood, and the sophisticated setting provides an elegant backdrop for a memorable dining experience.

Ox: Another Michelin-starred gem, Ox offers a contemporary dining experience with a focus on local produce and innovative techniques. The restaurant's tasting menu allows diners to explore a range of flavors and textures, making it a top choice for a special occasion or a culinary adventure.

CHAPTER 6

Outdoor and Adventure Activities

Hiking in the Scottish Highlands and Lake District

Scottish Highlands: The Scottish Highlands are renowned for their rugged beauty and diverse hiking opportunities. This region offers some of the most spectacular and challenging hikes in the UK. The iconic Ben Nevis, the highest peak in the British Isles, attracts hikers with its dramatic landscapes and panoramic views. The ascent to Ben Nevis is demanding, but the reward is a breathtaking vista of the surrounding mountains and valleys. For a less strenuous yet equally scenic option, the Isle of Skye provides an array of hiking trails through enchanting landscapes. The Quiraing, with its unique rock formations and sweeping views, is a favorite among hikers seeking a mix of adventure and natural beauty.

The Cairngorms National Park is another excellent destination for hiking enthusiasts. The park's diverse terrain includes rolling hills, ancient forests, and shimmering lochs. Trails like the one leading to the summit of Cairn Gorm offer panoramic views of the vast wilderness, while the more relaxed route around Loch an Eilein provides a serene experience with opportunities to spot wildlife.

Lake District: The Lake District in Cumbria is celebrated for its picturesque lakes, rolling hills, and charming villages. Scafell Pike, the highest mountain in England, offers a challenging climb with rewarding views of the surrounding fells and lakes. For a gentler hike, the circular route around Derwentwater provides stunning lake views and passes through tranquil woodlands and meadows. The Langdale Valley is another notable hiking area, known for its dramatic scenery and varied trails, including the ascent of Pike of Stickle.

The Lake District also boasts a range of walking paths suitable for all levels. The popular Tarn Hows circuit is a relatively easy walk that showcases the area's beautiful scenery, including serene tarns and lush woodlands. The valley of Buttermere offers a classic British hiking experience with its scenic lake and mountain backdrop, perfect for those seeking both tranquility and adventure.

Coastal Walks and National Parks

South West Coast Path: The South West Coast Path is one of the longest and most scenic coastal walks in the UK, stretching over 600 miles from Poole Harbour in Dorset to Minehead in Somerset. This trail offers stunning views of dramatic cliffs, sandy beaches, and picturesque seaside villages. Highlights include the rugged coastline of Cornwall's Land's End, the charming town of St. Ives, and the picturesque cliffs of Exmoor National Park. Along the way, walkers can explore historic sites, enjoy fresh seafood, and take in the beauty of coastal flora and fauna.

Northumberland Coast: The Northumberland Coast Area of Outstanding Natural Beauty (AONB) is known for its unspoiled beaches, dramatic dunes, and historic castles. The coastal path here offers stunning views of the North Sea and the opportunity to explore the remote and wild landscape. Highlights include the picturesque village of Bamburgh with its imposing castle and the serene beauty of Holy Island, accessible by a causeway and known for its rich history and natural beauty.

Snowdonia National Park: Snowdonia, located in North Wales, is a haven for outdoor enthusiasts. The park is home to Mount Snowdon, the highest peak in Wales, which can be ascended via several routes, including the popular Llanberis Path. The views from the summit are spectacular, encompassing rugged mountains, lush valleys, and distant coastlines. Snowdonia also offers a variety of other trails, from the gentle walk around Llyn Idwal to the challenging ascent of Tryfan.

Yorkshire Dales National Park: The Yorkshire Dales National Park is characterized by its rolling hills, picturesque valleys, and charming stone villages. The park offers a range of hiking opportunities, including the classic Three Peaks Challenge, which involves climbing Pen-y-Ghent, Whernside, and Ingleborough. For a more relaxed experience, the walk along the Swale Trail provides beautiful views of the Swale Valley and its rivers.

Wildlife Watching and Outdoor Adventures

Scottish Wildlife: Scotland is renowned for its rich wildlife and opportunities for outdoor adventures. The Cairngorms National Park is a prime location for spotting native species such as red deer, golden eagles, and Scottish wildcats. The island of Mull is another excellent destination for wildlife enthusiasts, offering sightings of otters, puffins, and white-tailed sea eagles. The RSPB reserve at Loch Garten is famous for its osprey nest and provides a great opportunity to observe these magnificent birds in their natural habitat.

Lake District Wildlife: The Lake District is home to a variety of wildlife, including red squirrels, peregrine falcons, and roe deer. The area around Ullswater is particularly known for its wildlife, with opportunities to spot birds such as the curlew and the lapwing. The nature reserves around the lakes offer guided walks and educational programs for those interested in learning more about the local flora and fauna.

Wales Wildlife: In Wales, the Pembrokeshire Coast National Park is a haven for wildlife watchers. The park's coastal cliffs are breeding grounds for seabirds such as puffins and razorbills. The coastal path offers opportunities to spot seals and dolphins, particularly in the waters around Ramsey Island. The Bannau Brycheiniog National Park is another excellent location for wildlife, with its diverse habitats supporting species such as the red kite and the otter.

Northern Ireland Wildlife: Northern Ireland's Mourne Mountains are ideal for outdoor adventures and wildlife watching. The area is known for its diverse habitats, including heathlands and bogs, which are home to species such as the Irish hare and the peregrine falcon. The coastal cliffs of the Causeway Coast also provide opportunities to observe seabirds and marine life, with the Giant's Causeway offering a unique geological landscape alongside its natural beauty.

Adventure Activities

Mountain Biking: The UK offers numerous locations for mountain biking enthusiasts, from the rugged trails of the Scottish Highlands to the challenging tracks of the Lake District. The Fort William Mountain Bike World Cup track in Scotland is renowned for its downhill runs and technical sections. The Bike Park Wales in the Brecon Beacons provides a range of trails suitable for all levels, including downhill and cross-country routes.

Rock Climbing: For rock climbing, the UK has a variety of renowned locations. The Peak District offers classic climbs and bouldering opportunities, with popular spots like Stanage Edge and Frogatt Edge. In North Wales, the Llanberis Pass provides challenging routes and stunning scenery. The Lake District also features excellent climbing spots, including Borrowdale and Langdale.

Coasteering: Coasteering is an adventurous activity that combines climbing, swimming, and jumping along coastal rocks. The Pembrokeshire Coast National Park is a popular destination for coasteering, offering guided tours that explore sea caves, rock pools, and rugged coastlines. The North Coast of Northern Ireland, around the Giant's Causeway, also provides thrilling coasteering experiences with dramatic sea cliffs and rocky outcrops.

Kayaking and Canoeing: The UK's lakes, rivers, and coastlines offer ample opportunities for kayaking and canoeing. The Lake District's lakes, including Windermere and Coniston Water, are perfect for leisurely paddling and exploring picturesque scenery. In Scotland, the lochs and rivers provide a range of kayaking experiences, from serene lake paddles to adventurous river runs. The Welsh coastline offers opportunities for sea kayaking, with stunning views and access to hidden coves and caves.

Zip Lining: For a high-flying adventure, try zip lining at one of the UK's premier zip line locations. Zip World in Snowdonia features the world's longest zip line, Velocity 2, which offers an exhilarating ride over the stunning Welsh landscape. The Eden Project in Cornwall also offers an exciting zip line experience through its iconic biomes.

Surfing: The UK's coastlines offer great surfing opportunities, particularly in areas like Cornwall and Devon. Fistral Beach in Newquay is a popular surfing destination, known for its consistent waves and surf schools. In Scotland, Thurso provides challenging waves for experienced surfers, while the Gower Peninsula in Wales is known for its scenic surf spots.

UK Adventure Tips

1. Understand the Weather: The UK's weather can be highly variable, especially in mountainous and coastal regions. Always check the forecast before setting out and prepare for sudden changes. Pack layers, waterproofs, and weather-appropriate gear to stay comfortable and safe.

2. Plan Your Adventure: Thoroughly research your chosen activities and trails. Understand their difficulty levels, distances, and terrain to ensure they match your fitness and skill level. For longer hikes or remote adventures, inform someone of your plans and estimated return time.

3. Prioritize Safety: Carry a map, compass, or GPS device, and ensure you know how to use them. Equip yourself with a first-aid kit and be familiar with basic first-aid procedures. Be aware of local hazards, such as unstable terrain, wildlife, or strong currents.

4. Respect the Environment: Follow Leave No Trace principles to minimize your impact. Stick to marked trails, avoid disturbing wildlife, and carry out all litter. Be especially mindful in protected areas like national parks and nature reserves.

5. Stay Hydrated and Energized: Bring plenty of water and high-energy snacks to maintain your energy levels. For longer excursions, plan your meals and carry sufficient provisions. In areas with limited amenities, ensure you are well-stocked before you head out.

6. Check Your Gear: Ensure your equipment is in good condition before starting activities like climbing, kayaking, or mountain biking. For rentals, choose reputable providers. Regularly inspect your personal gear for wear and tear, and make repairs or replacements as needed.

7. Know Local Wildlife: Understand the wildlife in the area you're visiting and how to interact with it safely. In regions with large animals or specific ecological concerns, follow recommended safety guidelines. Be aware of tides and currents for water-based activities.

8. Consider Guided Tours: If you're unfamiliar with an area or activity, joining a guided tour can enhance your experience. Local guides provide valuable insights into the best spots, safety tips, and cultural or ecological information.

9. Secure Travel Insurance: Obtain travel insurance that covers adventure activities. This provides peace of mind in case of accidents, injuries, or equipment loss. Verify that your policy includes coverage for the specific activities you plan to undertake.

10. Follow Local Regulations: Adhere to local rules and regulations for outdoor activities. Some areas may require permits, have restricted access during certain seasons, or have guidelines for wildlife interactions.

11. Embrace Local Culture: Take the time to understand and respect local customs and traditions.

Engaging with local communities and appreciating their connection to the land can enrich your adventure.

12. Capture the Experience: Bring a camera or smartphone to document your journey, but be considerate of where and when it's appropriate to take photos. Respect private property and observe any restrictions on drone use.

13. Stay Updated: Keep informed about local news and advisories, especially if venturing into remote areas. This includes weather conditions, trail closures, and any safety warnings that might affect your plans.

14. Pack Efficiently: Pack essential gear and clothing without overloading your backpack. Opt for versatile items suited to varying weather conditions, ensuring you are well-prepared but not burdened.

15. Enjoy the Adventure: While preparation and safety are crucial, don't forget to savor the experience. Take time to appreciate the natural beauty around you and the unique experiences each destination offers.

Packing Tips for UK Adventures

1. Dress in Layers: The UK's weather is known for its unpredictability. Pack layers that you can easily add or remove. Start with moisture-wicking base layers, add insulating mid-layers like fleece or wool, and finish with a waterproof and windproof outer layer. This approach allows you to adjust your clothing based on changing conditions.

2. Choose Waterproof Gear: Invest in a high-quality, breathable waterproof jacket and pants to protect against rain and wind. Waterproof footwear, such as boots with sealed seams or gaiters, will keep your feet dry and comfortable in wet conditions.

3. Wear Comfortable Footwear: Select durable, comfortable footwear suited to the terrain you'll be exploring. For rugged trails, sturdy, waterproof hiking boots are ideal. For less demanding walks, well-cushioned trail shoes or walking shoes will suffice.

4. Pack a Functional Daypack: Carry a daypack with essential items, including a map, compass or GPS, a first-aid kit, a multitool, and an emergency whistle. Don't forget a hydration system (such as water bottles or a hydration bladder) and high-energy snacks to keep you fueled.

5. Protect Yourself from the Sun: Even on overcast days, UV rays can be strong. Pack sun protection essentials like sunscreen, sunglasses, and a hat to shield yourself from sunburn.

6. Ensure Personal Comfort: Bring lightweight, quick-drying clothing for comfort during activities. Consider packing a travel pillow and a lightweight blanket for extra comfort during long journeys or overnight stays.

7. Include Navigation Tools: While a GPS device is helpful, always carry a traditional map and compass as a backup. Familiarize yourself with navigation landmarks in the area.

8. Prepare for Emergencies: Equip yourself with a headlamp or flashlight, extra batteries, a fire-starting kit, and a multi-tool. These items can be crucial for safety and convenience in unexpected situations.

9. Maintain Hygiene: Pack personal hygiene essentials like hand sanitizer, toilet paper, and a small trowel if you're heading into areas without facilities. Remember to bring any personal medications or health supplies you may need.

10. Bring Camera Gear: If you plan to document your adventure, include a camera with extra batteries and memory cards. A waterproof case or pouch is useful if you'll be near water or in wet conditions.

11. Carry Important Documents: Keep essential documents such as identification, insurance details, and any permits or bookings in a waterproof pouch to protect them from the elements.

12. Use Eco-Friendly Products: Opt for reusable and eco-friendly items, such as water bottles, food containers, and shopping bags. Reducing waste helps preserve the natural beauty of the areas you visit.

Budget Advice for UK Adventures

1. Plan Ahead and Book Early: To secure the best rates and availability, book your accommodation, transportation, and activities well in advance. Early bookings often come with discounts and promotional offers that can help you save money.

2. Set a Realistic Budget: Before you embark on your trip, create a detailed budget that includes accommodation, transportation, food, activities, and a contingency for unexpected expenses. Keep in mind currency exchange rates and any additional costs, such as park entry fees or guided tours.

3. Opt for Budget Accommodation: Consider staying in budget-friendly options like hostels, guesthouses, or budget hotels. Camping is also a cost-effective choice, especially in scenic areas or national parks. Platforms like Airbnb can provide affordable and unique lodging options.

4. Explore Free or Low-Cost Activities: The UK boasts numerous free or low-cost attractions, including museums, galleries, and natural landmarks. Take advantage of city parks, coastal walks, and hiking trails, which often have no admission fees.

5. Use Discount Passes and Offers: Look into city passes or discount cards that provide reduced entry fees to multiple attractions. Many cities offer visitor passes that include savings on transportation, dining, and attractions.

6. Rely on Public Transportation: Opt for public transport such as buses, trains, and trams, which are generally more affordable than taxis or car rentals. Consider purchasing travel passes or cards for unlimited journeys within certain areas.

7. Travel Off-Peak: Avoid peak tourist seasons and holidays to benefit from lower prices on flights, accommodation, and attractions. Traveling during off-peak times can lead to substantial savings.

8. Prepare Your Own Meals: Save money on dining by shopping at local markets or grocery stores and preparing your own meals. Many hostels and accommodations offer kitchen facilities, and picnicking can be a cost-effective and enjoyable way to eat.

9. Set a Budget for Souvenirs: Allocate a specific amount for souvenirs and gifts. Shop at local markets and smaller shops for unique items at reasonable prices, and be mindful of expensive tourist souvenirs.

10. Monitor Your Spending: Keep track of your expenses throughout your trip to ensure you stay within your budget. Use budgeting apps or a simple spreadsheet to manage your spending and make adjustments as needed.

11. Invest in Travel Insurance: Although it may seem like an additional expense, travel insurance can be a cost-saving measure in the event of health issues, cancellations, or lost belongings, offering financial protection and peace of mind.

12. Seek Local Deals and Discounts: Check local tourism websites or visitor centers for current deals and discounts on attractions and dining. Many places offer special promotions or discounts to visitors.

13. Consider Alternative Transportation: For shorter distances, biking or walking can be both enjoyable and economical ways to explore cities and scenic areas, reducing your reliance on more expensive forms of transport.

14. Utilize Loyalty Programs: If you frequently stay with specific hotel chains or use certain airlines, leverage loyalty programs to earn rewards and benefits that can help reduce your travel costs.

15. Be Flexible with Your Plans: Flexibility can lead to significant savings. Adjusting your itinerary based on availability and price changes can help you take advantage of last-minute deals and offers.

CHAPTER 7

Shopping in the United Kingdom

London's Luxury Shopping and Boutiques

London is renowned for its high-end shopping experiences, offering an array of luxury stores and exclusive boutiques.

Bond Street: Known as London's premier luxury shopping destination, Bond Street is home to world-famous brands such as Cartier, Chanel, and Louis Vuitton. The street is lined with elegant storefronts and showcases the latest in haute couture and fine jewelry. It's a must-visit for those seeking high-end fashion and luxury goods.

Harrods: Located in Knightsbridge, Harrods is an iconic department store offering a lavish shopping experience. The store features a diverse range of luxury products, from designer clothing and accessories to gourmet food and fine wines. The grandeur of its architecture and opulent interior make it a unique shopping destination.

Selfridges: Situated on Oxford Street, Selfridges is another top department store known for its impressive range of high-end fashion, beauty products, and home goods. The store often hosts exclusive collections and designer collaborations, providing a dynamic shopping experience.

Westfield London: For those seeking a blend of luxury and high street shopping, Westfield London in White City offers an extensive selection of designer boutiques and flagship stores. The shopping center also features a range of dining options and entertainment facilities, making it a comprehensive retail destination.

Savile Row: Famous for bespoke tailoring, Savile Row is the place to find custom-made suits and high-quality menswear. Esteemed tailors such as Henry Poole & Co and Gieves & Hawkes offer a tradition of craftsmanship and luxury that has made Savile Row a name synonymous with bespoke fashion.

Local Markets and Artisan Shops

Beyond the luxury boutiques, the UK boasts a wealth of local markets and artisan shops, each offering unique products and a taste of local culture.

Borough Market: Located near London Bridge, Borough Market is one of London's oldest and most renowned food markets. It features a diverse range of gourmet foods, fresh produce, and artisanal products. Visitors can sample and purchase everything from handmade cheeses and cured meats to fresh bread and international street food.

Portobello Road Market: Situated in Notting Hill, Portobello Road Market is famous for its eclectic mix of antiques, vintage clothing, and fresh produce. The market operates throughout the week, with the busiest and most vibrant trading day being Saturday. It's an excellent place to find unique items and immerse yourself in a lively market atmosphere.

Camden Market: Known for its alternative and eclectic vibe, Camden Market offers a variety of stalls selling handmade crafts, vintage clothing, and unique accessories. The market is a hotspot for quirky finds and independent designer goods, making it a great place for those seeking something different.

Bath's Artisan Shops: In the historic city of Bath, local artisan shops offer a range of handcrafted goods, from bespoke jewelry to artisanal soaps and candles. The city's charming boutiques provide a more personalized shopping experience and showcase the skills of local craftsmen and women.

Edinburgh's Royal Mile: The Royal Mile in Edinburgh is lined with traditional Scottish shops and craft stores. Visitors can find an array of Scottish goods, including tartan clothing, whisky, and handmade souvenirs. The historic setting adds to the charm of shopping along this iconic street.

Best Places to Buy Souvenirs

When it comes to souvenirs, the UK offers a variety of options that capture the essence of your visit.

Souvenir Shops in Historic Cities: In cities like Edinburgh, York, and Oxford, souvenir shops offer a range of items from traditional British memorabilia to local artisanal crafts. Look for items such as historical replicas, local artwork, and unique keepsakes that reflect the city's heritage.

Tourist Attractions and Museums: Many tourist attractions and museums, such as the British Museum and the Tower of London, have gift shops with a selection of themed souvenirs. These can include replica artifacts, museum-branded merchandise, and educational toys.

Tea Shops and British Cuisine Stores: Purchase traditional British tea, biscuits, and jams from specialty tea shops and British food stores. These make for delightful souvenirs and offer a taste of British culinary culture.

Local Artisans and Craftspeople: For more unique and handcrafted items, visit local artisans and craft fairs. Products such as handmade pottery, bespoke jewelry, and locally produced textiles offer a personal touch and support local craftsmanship.

Historic Pubs and Inns: Some historic pubs and inns offer branded merchandise, including pint glasses, coasters, and shirts. These can serve as fun and memorable souvenirs of your visit to a traditional British pub.

How to Avoid Common Scams

1. Be Cautious with Money:

Avoid Overcharging: When using taxis or ride-sharing services, agree on the fare before starting the journey or use a meter. Be cautious of unofficial taxis that might overcharge.

Watch for Fake Currency: When exchanging money, use authorized money changers or banks. Check the currency carefully for authenticity and avoid exchanging large sums in unfamiliar locations.

2. Beware of Unofficial Tours:

Book Through Reputable Sources: Research and book tours through reputable travel agencies or platforms. Avoid deals that seem too good to be true or operators without proper licenses.

Verify Prices and Inclusions: Confirm what is included in the tour price, such as entry fees, meals, and transportation. Ensure there are no hidden costs before making any payments.

3. Protect Personal Belongings:

Keep Valuables Safe: Use a hotel safe or a secure travel pouch to keep important items like passports, cash, and electronics safe. Avoid carrying large amounts of cash or valuables in public.

Avoid Flashing Valuables: Be discreet with expensive items like jewelry and high-end electronics. Keeping valuables out of sight helps prevent theft or unwanted attention.

4. Stay Informed:

Local Advice: Seek advice from locals, your accommodation, or trusted sources if you're unsure about any aspect of your travel. Locals can provide valuable insights and help you avoid potential issues.

Emergency Contacts: Keep a list of emergency contacts, including local authorities, your embassy or consulate, and your accommodation. Having these contacts readily available ensures you can quickly address any issues that arise.

5. Common Scams:

Types of Scams: Detail common scams specific to Bali and Komodo Island, such as overcharging for tours, fake charity collectors, or timeshare presentations.

How to Recognize: Tips on how to recognize and avoid these scams can be beneficial, such as being cautious of deals that require immediate payment or offers that seem unusually low.

6. Reporting Issues:

Report Scams: Provide information on how to report scams or fraud to local authorities or your embassy. Include contact details for local police or consumer protection agencies.

7. Safety Precautions:

Safe Practices: Emphasize safe practices such as avoiding walking alone at night in unfamiliar areas, and keeping your accommodation and travel arrangements well-documented and verified.

Best Shopping Tips for the UK

1. Understand Sale Seasons: The UK has specific sale periods where significant discounts are available. Key sale times include the Boxing Day sales (26th December) and the January sales, as well as summer sales starting in late June or early July. Shopping during these times can yield substantial savings.

2. Claim VAT Refunds: As a non-EU visitor, you can claim a VAT (Value Added Tax) refund on certain purchases. Look for stores that offer VAT refunds, and request a VAT refund form with your purchase. Ensure you get the form stamped at the airport before departing the UK.

3. Utilize Loyalty Programs and Apps: Many UK retailers offer loyalty cards and mobile apps that provide discounts, rewards, and exclusive offers. Signing up for these programs can give you access to promotions and accumulate points for future savings.

4. Explore Outlet Stores: Outlet centers are a great way to find discounted designer and high-street brands. Popular outlets such as Bicester Village near Oxford and McArthurGlen Designer Outlet in London offer significant savings on a wide range of brands.

5. Take Advantage of Duty-Free Shopping: If you're traveling internationally, use duty-free shops at airports to purchase luxury items and other goods at reduced prices due to exemption from local taxes.

6. Compare Prices Online: Before making a purchase, compare prices online to ensure you're getting the best deal. Many UK retailers offer exclusive online discounts, and comparison websites can help you find the best prices across different stores.

7. Visit Local Markets: Discover unique and often more affordable items at local markets. Markets like Borough Market in London and the Edinburgh Farmers' Market offer fresh produce, artisanal goods, and distinctive finds not typically available in traditional stores.

8. Watch for Special Offers and Promotions: Keep an eye out for special promotions such as buy-one-get-one-free offers, multi-buy discounts, and limited-time sales. Retailers often advertise these deals through in-store signage, their websites, and social media.

9. Support Independent Shops: Explore independent and boutique stores for unique items and handcrafted goods. These shops often provide personalized service and distinctive products that you won't find in chain stores.

10. Bring a Reusable Bag: Many UK retailers charge for plastic bags. To save money and reduce environmental impact, bring your own reusable shopping bag.

11. Be Aware of Exchange Rates: If using foreign currency, be mindful of exchange rates and potential fees for currency conversion. Opt for credit cards that offer favorable exchange rates and no foreign transaction fees to minimize conversion costs.

12. Familiarize Yourself with Store Policies: Understand return and exchange policies before making a purchase. UK stores often have specific policies, and knowing these can help you make informed decisions and avoid complications later.

13. Look for Additional Discounts: Some retailers may offer further discounts for cash payments or during specific promotional periods. Inquire about any potential VAT exemptions or additional savings available at checkout.

14. Bargain in Markets: In markets selling antiques or vintage items, bargaining is often acceptable. Don't hesitate to negotiate prices politely to secure a better deal.

15. Stay Informed on Shopping Trends: Follow fashion and shopping blogs, local magazines, and social media to stay updated on the latest trends, new store openings, and exclusive shopping events in the UK.

CHAPTER 8

Accommodations: Where to Stay in the UK

Luxury Hotels and Boutique Stays

The UK is renowned for its exceptional luxury hotels and boutique accommodations, each offering a unique blend of opulence and charm.

In London, The Ritz stands as an epitome of classic luxury. Nestled in the heart of the city, this prestigious hotel has been serving high society and celebrities since 1906. Guests are treated to lavishly decorated rooms, a world-class dining experience, and impeccable service that makes for an unforgettable stay. The Ritz's elegant ballroom and renowned afternoon tea are highlights of the experience.

Another iconic choice is Claridge's in Mayfair, known for its timeless elegance and modern comforts. The hotel's art deco design and exquisite dining options offer a sophisticated atmosphere. Claridge's is also famous for its afternoon tea, a British tradition that guests can enjoy in a setting of luxury and grandeur.

For those venturing to Scotland, The Balmoral in Edinburgh provides a majestic experience with its stunning views of the city and Edinburgh Castle. The hotel's Scottish charm is reflected in its beautifully appointed rooms and its Michelin-starred restaurant, which serves contemporary Scottish cuisine.

In London, The Savoy offers an illustrious blend of historic charm and modern luxury. Overlooking the Thames, this hotel is celebrated for its opulent rooms, high-end dining options, and a rich history of hosting celebrities and dignitaries. Its striking Edwardian and Art Deco architecture further enhances its appeal.

Boutique hotels offer a more personalized and distinctive experience. The Hoxton in Shoreditch, London, is known for its trendy and contemporary style. The hotel's design incorporates vibrant colors and stylish furnishings, creating a lively and modern atmosphere. The Hoxton also boasts a popular restaurant and communal spaces that encourage social interaction.

The Zetter Townhouse, also in London, is a charming boutique hotel known for its eclectic decor and intimate ambiance. Each room is uniquely designed with vintage furnishings and quirky touches, offering a warm and memorable stay in the heart of the city.

In Chester, The Chester Grosvenor blends historic charm with modern luxury. The hotel's elegant rooms and its Michelin-starred restaurant provide a refined experience, complemented by its prime location for exploring Chester's historic streets and landmarks.

Budget-Friendly Options

For travelers seeking more affordable accommodation without sacrificing comfort, the UK offers a variety of budget-friendly options.

Premier Inn provides a reliable and economical choice with numerous locations across the UK. The hotel chain offers comfortable rooms with modern amenities at competitive prices, making it a great option for budget-conscious travelers. Premier Inn's consistent quality ensures a pleasant stay without the luxury price tag.

Another popular budget option is Travelodge, known for its straightforward and affordable accommodations. With numerous locations throughout the UK, Travelodge provides no-frills, comfortable lodging ideal for travelers seeking basic amenities and value for money.

YHA (Youth Hostels Association) hostels offer a more economical and social option for travelers. With locations spanning urban centers and scenic countryside, YHA hostels provide clean and affordable lodging with a friendly atmosphere. These hostels are particularly suited for younger travelers or those seeking a communal experience.

Guesthouses and bed-and-breakfasts offer a more intimate and often less expensive alternative to traditional hotels. For instance, The Coach House features family-run guesthouses with cozy rooms and hearty breakfasts, providing a homely and welcoming environment at a reasonable price. Similarly, The White House offers comfortable bed-and-breakfast accommodations with delicious breakfasts and personalized service.

Unique Stays: Castles, Cottages, and More

For a truly distinctive lodging experience, consider staying in unique accommodations that offer a blend of history, charm, and adventure.

Staying in castles provides a regal and memorable experience. Ashford Castle in County Mayo, Ireland, offers a luxurious stay with its grand rooms, stunning grounds, and a range of activities such as falconry and horseback riding. The castle's rich history and opulent interiors create a fairy-tale setting for a truly special stay.

In the South of France, the Château de Fonscolombe combines historic charm with modern luxury. Guests can enjoy the castle's elegant rooms, beautiful gardens, and fine dining in a setting that evokes a sense of timeless sophistication.

Countryside cottages offer a cozy and serene retreat from city life. In the Cotswolds, charming cottages provide a quintessentially English experience with picturesque views, quaint villages, and traditional rural life. These cottages offer a homely atmosphere and easy access to scenic walking trails and local attractions.

In the Lake District, cabin and cottage accommodations offer a tranquil escape amidst stunning natural landscapes. These properties provide a private and peaceful setting, ideal for enjoying outdoor activities such as hiking and boating, while also providing a comfortable base from which to explore the region's natural beauty.

Unique accommodations include options such as glamping, houseboats, and treehouses. Glamping sites across the UK offer a luxurious take on camping, with well-appointed tents featuring stylish interiors and modern amenities. This experience combines the charm of outdoor living with the comforts of a hotel stay.

Houseboats in cities like London and Edinburgh offer a charming and unconventional lodging option. Staying on the water provides unique views and a distinctive living experience, with the added benefit of being centrally located.

For a whimsical and adventurous stay, consider booking a treehouse accommodation. Nestled in woodlands or gardens, these treehouses offer a fun and immersive experience, with elevated views and a connection to nature that adds an extra layer of excitement to your stay.

Sample Budget for Accommodations in the UK

Luxury Hotels and Boutique Stays

In London, **The Ritz** is a symbol of classic luxury, with an average cost per night ranging from £500 to £1,000. Known for its opulent rooms, exquisite dining options, and impeccable service, The Ritz offers a truly lavish experience. Prices can fluctuate based on the season and room type.

Another prestigious option is **Claridge's**, located in Mayfair. This hotel combines timeless elegance with modern comforts, with nightly rates between £400 and £800. Guests can enjoy elegant rooms, a renowned afternoon tea, and luxury amenities. Rates may vary with special packages or seasonal promotions.

In Edinburgh, **The Balmoral** provides a majestic stay with its stunning views of the city and Edinburgh Castle. Prices typically range from £300 to £600 per night. The hotel's Scottish charm, Michelin-starred dining, and refined atmosphere make it a top choice for a luxurious experience. Rates may increase during festivals or peak tourist seasons.

The Savoy, another historic luxury hotel in London, offers a blend of grandeur and modern luxury, with average costs ranging from £400 to £750 per night. Overlooking the Thames, it boasts opulent rooms, high-end dining, and a rich history. Booking in advance might help secure better rates.

Budget-Friendly Options

For those on a tighter budget, **Premier Inn** offers a reliable and economical option, with prices ranging from £50 to £100 per night. With numerous locations across the UK, Premier Inn provides comfortable rooms and modern amenities at a competitive price. Costs can be lower with early bookings or during off-peak periods.

Travelodge is another popular choice for budget accommodation, with nightly rates between £40 and £80.

Known for its straightforward and affordable lodgings, Travelodge offers good value for money, and special offers or advance bookings can further reduce costs.

The **Youth Hostels Association (YHA)** operates a network of hostels across the UK, with prices ranging from £20 to £60 for a bed in a shared dorm. These hostels are ideal for budget travelers seeking clean facilities and a social atmosphere. Private rooms are available at higher rates.

Guesthouses and bed-and-breakfasts provide a more intimate and often less expensive alternative to traditional hotels. The average cost per night is between £60 and £120. Places like The Coach House offer charming, family-run guesthouses with cozy rooms and hearty breakfasts, while The White House provides a welcoming bed-and-breakfast experience with delicious morning meals.

Unique Stays: Castles, Cottages, and More

For a unique lodging experience, staying in a castle such as **Ashford Castle** in County Mayo, Ireland, offers a blend of luxury and history. Average nightly rates range from £300 to £700, with guests enjoying grand rooms, stunning grounds, and activities like falconry and horseback riding. Rates can vary based on room type and season.

In the South of France, the **Château de Fonscolombe** combines historic charm with modern luxury, with rates ranging from €250 to €600 (approximately £215 to £515) per night. This accommodation offers elegant rooms, beautiful gardens, and fine dining, with prices potentially increasing during peak tourist seasons.

Countryside cottages provide a cozy and serene retreat, with average costs ranging from £100 to £250 per night. In the Cotswolds, charming cottages offer picturesque views and a traditional rural experience. In the Lake District, cabin accommodations range from £80 to £200 per night, providing a peaceful setting amidst natural beauty.

For a whimsical stay, **glamping sites** offer luxury camping with prices between £100 and £250 per night. These sites feature well-appointed tents with stylish interiors and modern amenities, providing a unique outdoor experience. Rates can be higher for more luxurious setups or during peak periods.

Houseboats in cities like London and Edinburgh provide a charming and unconventional lodging option, with nightly rates ranging from £100 to £250. Staying on the water offers unique views and a distinctive experience, with rates depending on location, size, and amenities.

For an adventurous and whimsical experience, **treehouses** offer elevated views and a close connection to nature, with costs ranging from £150 to £300 per night. Prices can vary based on location, size, and luxury level, making treehouses a fun and immersive lodging choice.

1. London's Luxury Shopping and Boutiques

- **Harrods**
  Address: 87-135 Brompton Road, Knightsbridge, London SW1X 7XL, UK
- **Selfridges**
  Address: 400 Oxford Street, London W1A 1AB, UK
- **Liberty London**
  Address: Regent Street, London W1B 5AH, UK

2. Local Markets and Artisan Shops

- **Borough Market** (London)
  Address: 8 Southwark Street, London SE1 1TL, UK
- **Camden Market** (London)
  Address: Camden Lock Place, London NW1 8AF, UK
- **Portobello Road Market** (London)
  Address: Portobello Road, London W11 1LJ, UK

3. Best Places to Buy Souvenirs

- **Edinburgh's Royal Mile**

  Address: The Royal Mile, Edinburgh, EH1 1PE, UK
- **The Shambles** (York)

  Address: The Shambles, York YO1 7LZ, UK
- **The Lanes** (Brighton)

  Address: The Lanes, Brighton BN1 1HB, UK

CHAPTER 9

Transportation and Getting Around

Getting around the United Kingdom is generally efficient, thanks to its well-developed transportation networks. Whether you're traveling across the country or exploring cities and rural areas, you'll find a variety of options to suit different preferences and budgets. From the extensive train system to convenient buses and driving opportunities, this chapter provides insights on how to navigate the UK like a local.

Public Transportation: Trains, Buses, and More

The public transportation system in the UK is both comprehensive and reliable, making it a preferred option for locals and visitors alike. Trains, buses, and underground metro systems offer convenient access to cities, towns, and rural areas.

The **rail network** is one of the most efficient ways to travel between cities and regions. **National Rail** services connect major cities such as London, Edinburgh, Manchester, Birmingham, and Cardiff, providing fast and frequent trains. For instance, the journey from London to Edinburgh takes around four to five hours on a high-speed train, while a trip from London to Manchester typically takes just over two hours. **Virgin Trains**, **Great Western Railway**, and **LNER (London North Eastern Railway)** are some of the prominent rail operators offering comfortable services with amenities like Wi-Fi, refreshments, and onboard entertainment.

One notable option for those traveling extensively by train is the **BritRail Pass**, which offers unlimited train travel across the UK for a set number of days. This can be a cost-effective solution for tourists planning to visit multiple destinations over a short period. The pass is available for various durations, making it easy to customize your travel plans.

London's underground system, commonly known as the **Tube**, is an iconic way to get around the city. With 11 lines crisscrossing the capital, the Tube offers quick and frequent access to virtually every part of London. Oyster cards or contactless payment methods are the easiest and most cost-effective ways to pay for Tube journeys. The London Underground operates from early morning to late at night, with some lines running 24 hours on weekends.

Outside of London, major cities like **Edinburgh**, **Glasgow**, and **Manchester** have their own urban transportation networks, including **buses**, **trams**, and **local trains**. In Edinburgh, the **Lothian Buses** network is extensive and connects all corners of the city. In Manchester, the **Metrolink tram system** is an efficient way to navigate the city and surrounding areas.

Buses are another affordable and convenient mode of transport for both short and long-distance travel.

National Express and **Megabus** are two major coach operators offering services between cities at very reasonable prices. Buses tend to be slower than trains but are ideal for budget-conscious travelers or those looking for a more scenic route. In cities, local bus services run frequently, providing access to neighborhoods and suburbs that may not be covered by train or tram networks.

Renting a Car and Driving in the UK

For travelers who prefer flexibility and the freedom to explore off-the-beaten-path destinations, renting a car is a great option. While public transport is well-suited for city and regional travel, rural areas, scenic drives, and remote attractions are often best accessed by car.

Renting a car in the UK is straightforward, with several international and local rental companies available, including **Avis**, **Enterprise**, **Hertz**, and **Europcar**. You can rent a car from airports, major train stations, and city centers. It's recommended to book in advance, especially during peak tourist seasons, to secure the best rates and availability. Most rental companies require drivers to be at least 21 years old, though some may have higher age limits or charge a surcharge for younger drivers.

Driving in the UK is on the **left-hand side** of the road, which may require some adjustment if you're from a country where driving is on the right. Roundabouts are common, and it's important to give way to traffic coming from the right. The road signage is clear, and GPS or mobile navigation apps make it easy to find your way.

One of the most scenic driving routes is along the **Scottish Highlands**. Renting a car to drive the **North Coast 500** is a fantastic way to experience some of Scotland's most breathtaking landscapes, from rugged coastlines to tranquil lochs and mountains. Similarly, driving through the **Lake District** offers beautiful views of rolling hills, lakes, and charming villages.

In terms of costs, fuel in the UK is generally more expensive compared to the US, with prices often fluctuating depending on the region. Fuel is sold by the liter, and petrol stations are widely available. Renting a fuel-efficient car can help keep costs down, and opting for a diesel vehicle may offer better mileage.

Parking in cities like London can be challenging and expensive. It's advisable to use public transport for city exploration and only rent a car for countryside or regional trips. Many UK cities have **park-and-ride** systems, where you can leave your car in a designated parking lot outside the city center and take public transport into the city. This option is often more convenient and affordable.

Tips for Navigating Cities and Countryside

Navigating UK cities and the countryside requires different approaches, depending on where you are and how you're traveling.

In cities like London, using public transportation such as the Tube, buses, and trains is the most efficient way to get around. London's streets can be congested, especially during peak hours, making driving less practical. If you prefer to explore on foot, cities like Edinburgh and Bath offer compact layouts, allowing you to discover attractions at your own pace. For added convenience, cities have well-marked pedestrian routes and frequent bus services.

If you plan to travel between cities, **train travel** is often the quickest and most convenient option. The UK's extensive train network connects even the most remote towns and villages, making it easy to hop from one destination to another without worrying about driving or parking.

In the countryside, having a **car** can be a huge advantage, especially when exploring rural areas or scenic regions like the Scottish Highlands, the Lake District, or Wales. Many rural attractions are not accessible by public transport, and driving allows you to take in the stunning landscapes at your own pace. That said, country roads can be narrow and winding, so it's important to drive cautiously, especially in remote areas where livestock or wildlife may be present on the roads.

For more adventurous travelers, **cycling** is an excellent way to explore the UK's countryside. National Cycle Routes offer scenic paths for cyclists, providing a slow and immersive experience. For example, cycling through **Cornwall's coastal roads** or the **Cotswolds' rolling hills** allows you to take in the stunning views while engaging in a physically rewarding activity.

When navigating cities or rural areas, having a **transport app** such as **Google Maps** or **Citymapper** can make a big difference. These apps provide real-time public transportation updates, directions, and journey times, ensuring you get where you need to go with minimal hassle. You can also purchase transportation tickets through some apps, making your journey smoother.

Local Transit: Navigating Cities with Ease

Each major city in the United Kingdom boasts its own local transit system, making it easy for travelers to get around without needing a car. Whether you're exploring the bustling streets of London, the historic lanes of Edinburgh, or the vibrant neighborhoods of Manchester, local transit options provide affordable and efficient ways to experience the cities.

In **London**, the public transportation system is iconic and comprehensive. The **London Underground**, or **Tube**, is the most convenient way to travel across the city. With 11 lines covering more than 250 stations, it connects virtually every part of London, from the city center to the suburbs. The Tube operates from early morning until midnight, with certain lines offering 24-hour service on weekends. Fares are based on travel zones, and using an **Oyster card** or **contactless payment** reduces costs compared to paper tickets.

London's **bus network** is equally extensive and operates 24/7. While buses are slower due to traffic, they offer a great way to see the city and are perfect for short trips or for areas not easily accessible by the Tube. The famous **red double-decker buses** are a quintessential part of the London experience. Most buses are cashless, so it's recommended to use an Oyster card or contactless payment.

For a scenic alternative, London's **riverboats** run along the Thames, offering stunning views of landmarks like the Tower of London, Westminster, and the London Eye. The **Uber Boat by Thames Clippers** operates as part of the city's transport network, allowing commuters and tourists to travel via the river while avoiding road congestion.

Outside London, cities like **Edinburgh, Glasgow**, and **Manchester** have well-established local transit systems.

In **Edinburgh**, **Lothian Buses** are the primary mode of transport. The buses are frequent, reliable, and cover the entire city and surrounding areas. For contactless payments, you can tap your card or phone on the bus, making travel easy. Edinburgh also has a **tram line** connecting the city center to the airport, passing through major shopping districts and suburbs.

Glasgow is served by the **Subway**, one of the world's oldest underground systems. Although small, with just one circular line, it efficiently connects key areas of the city. The city also has an extensive **bus network** operated by **First Glasgow**, and **trains** link Glasgow with nearby towns and suburbs.

In **Manchester**, the **Metrolink tram system** is the most popular mode of transportation. Covering the city center, suburbs, and even extending to nearby towns, it's a fast and efficient way to get around. Manchester's **buses** also provide an affordable and widespread service, while **trains** link the city with nearby destinations like Liverpool, Leeds, and Sheffield.

In **Birmingham**, the **West Midlands Metro** connects key areas of the city and nearby regions. The **local bus**

system is extensive and connects the suburbs to the city center, making it easy to navigate even without a car.

Smaller cities like **Bath**, **Brighton**, and **Cambridge** offer reliable local bus services. In seaside towns such as Brighton, buses are often the easiest way to explore the city and nearby attractions. In cities with compact layouts like Bath, walking is often the best way to get around, with buses and local train services filling the gap for longer trips.

Taxis and ride-sharing services such as **Uber**, **Bolt**, and **FreeNow** are also available in most UK cities. Black cabs are iconic in cities like London and are metered, while private hire vehicles like Uber offer app-based rides with clear fare estimates before booking. Taxi apps are especially useful for late-night trips or in areas not well-served by public transport.

Exploring Rural Areas by Local Transit

While public transport in cities is extensive, rural areas often have more limited transit options. However, regional buses and local trains can still provide access to many smaller towns and villages.

In places like the Lake District or Scottish Highlands, local bus services operate between villages and major towns, but they may run less frequently compared to city services. For example, in the Lake District, the Stagecoach bus service connects popular hiking destinations like Keswick, Ambleside, and Windermere. Planning ahead and checking bus timetables is essential when using public transport in rural areas.

In Wales, Arriva Trains Wales operates regional train services connecting the country's more remote regions, and local buses help fill in the gaps. Pembrokeshire, known for its rugged coastline and national park, has a seasonal Coastal Bus Service catering to visitors exploring the area's scenic trails and beaches.

For island destinations like the Isle of Skye, Caledonian MacBrayne (CalMac) offers ferry services from the mainland, and local bus services connect visitors to towns and landmarks once on the island. Rural buses tend to be less frequent, so renting a car or using local tour services may offer more flexibility for in-depth exploration

Travel Cards and Discount Options

For frequent travelers, using **travel cards** can provide significant savings. In London, the **Oyster card** is the most convenient way to pay for public transport, offering discounted fares on the Tube, buses, and trams. In other cities, similar contactless systems are available. For example, Edinburgh offers the **Ridacard**, providing unlimited travel on buses and trams.

Rail travelers can take advantage of discount cards such as the **Railcard**, which offers up to 1/3 off train fares.

There are different types of Railcards tailored to various age groups and travel needs, including the **16-25 Railcard**, the **Two Together Railcard**, and the **Senior Railcard**.

Sample Budget for Transportation and Getting Around the UK

When planning your transportation across the UK, it's important to consider the costs associated with different modes of travel. Below is a sample budget for a week-long trip, covering a mix of public transportation, car rentals, and other transit options.

For public transportation in London, using the Underground (Tube) and buses can cost around £7 to £10 per day with an Oyster card, or £14.90 per day for a Travelcard covering Zones 1-2. For unlimited travel for a week in Zones 1-2, the cost is approximately £41.20. For a week of public transportation in London, you can budget around £50 to £70.

Intercity train travel between major cities varies depending on how early you book. A one-way train from London to Edinburgh can cost between £50 to £100, while trips from London to Manchester range from £30 to £70. London to Bath tickets typically cost around £20 to £40 one way. For a week of intercity travel, budgeting £150 to £200 is reasonable.

Outside of London, local buses and trams are generally affordable. For instance, in Edinburgh or Manchester, local bus day passes cost around £4 to £5. The tram in Edinburgh, connecting the city center to the airport, costs £6.50 for a one-way trip. A weekly budget for local buses and trams in cities outside of London is around £20 to £40.

If you plan to rent a car, compact car rentals typically cost £25 to £40 per day, with weekly rentals ranging from £150 to £250. For a one-week rental with basic insurance, budgeting £200 to £250 is advisable. Fuel costs vary depending on driving distances, with petrol prices averaging £1.50 to £1.70 per liter. For moderate driving, expect to spend £60 to £80 on fuel for the week. Parking fees can add up, especially in urban areas, where it's common to pay £10 to £25 per day for parking. In more rural areas, parking tends to be free or much cheaper. A weekly budget for parking might be around £50 to £70.

Taxis and ride-sharing services such as Uber offer flexibility, with London black cab rides costing £10 to £20 for short trips and Uber rides between £7 and £15. In cities like Manchester or Edinburgh, taxi rides cost between £5 and £15, while Uber is slightly cheaper at around £5 to £10. For occasional taxi or ride-sharing use, budgeting £50 to £80 for the week should cover most needs.

To summarize, a week of transportation around the UK, including public transport, car rental, fuel, and occasional taxis or ride-shares, may cost between £580 and £790, depending on your specific travel preferences.

Expense	Estimated Cost
Public Transportation (Tube, Buses)	£50-70
Intercity Train Travel	£150-200
Local Buses/Trams Outside London	£20-40
Car Rental and Insurance	£200-250
Fuel Costs	£60-80
Parking Fees	£50-70
Taxis and Ride-Sharing	£50-80
Total Estimated Budget	**£580-790**

CHAPTER 10

Planning Your Budget: A Guide to Estimating Costs for Your UK Trip

Planning your budget for a trip to the United Kingdom is essential to ensure you make the most of your experience while keeping costs under control. From transportation and accommodation to dining and attractions, understanding how much to allocate for each aspect of your journey can help you avoid unexpected expenses and enjoy a stress-free vacation.

When budgeting for your trip, start by identifying the key components that will make up the bulk of your costs: flights, accommodation, transportation, food and drink, sightseeing, and personal expenses. Costs can vary greatly depending on the time of year, the regions you visit, and the type of experiences you prioritize.

Estimating Costs for Your Trip

The United Kingdom offers a range of experiences to suit various budgets, from luxury getaways to more affordable, budget-friendly adventures. To get a clearer idea of how much you might spend, let's break down the typical expenses:

Flights are likely to be one of the most significant expenses. Depending on your departure location, return flights to major UK cities like London, Manchester, or Edinburgh can range between £200 and £600 for economy class. Booking well in advance or using flight comparison tools can help secure lower fares. Consider flying into smaller airports or during off-peak seasons to save money.

Accommodation prices in the UK can vary widely. In London, mid-range hotels may cost between £100 and £200 per night, while luxury hotels could be upwards of £300 per night. However, in smaller cities like York, Bath, or Cardiff, mid-range accommodations can cost between £70 and £150 per night. Hostels and budget hotels offer more affordable options, typically costing £20 to £50 per night.

Transportation within the UK is generally affordable and efficient. For intra-city travel, expect to spend about £7 to £10 per day on public transport in London and slightly less in other cities. Train fares between cities can vary depending on the distance and booking in advance, with prices ranging from £20 to £100 per trip. Renting a car will add to your budget, with daily rates around £25 to £40, plus fuel and parking fees.

Dining out in the UK also depends on where you are and the type of establishment you choose. A meal at a mid-range restaurant could cost anywhere from £15 to £30 per person, while a pub meal or fast food might cost £8 to £12. Expect to spend more in cities like London, where prices are higher, while rural areas and smaller towns tend to offer more affordable dining options. For budget-conscious travelers, grocery stores and casual eateries like Pret A Manger offer affordable and tasty meals.

Sightseeing and attractions are part of what makes the UK so captivating. Many iconic attractions, such as the British Museum and National Gallery, are free to visit, especially in London. However, admission fees for other popular sites, such as Stonehenge, Edinburgh Castle, or the Tower of London, can cost between £10 and £30 per ticket. Consider investing in attraction passes like the London Pass or National Trust Membership, which can offer substantial savings if you plan to visit multiple paid attractions.

Shopping and souvenirs are additional costs to consider. Budget for souvenirs, especially if you're visiting local markets or iconic stores like Harrods. Expect to spend £10 to £50 on typical items like tea, local crafts, or clothing. If you plan to indulge in luxury shopping, prepare for higher costs.

Saving Money: Travel Hacks and Deals

Traveling to the UK doesn't have to break the bank if you take advantage of some travel hacks. With a little planning and research, you can significantly reduce your overall expenses without sacrificing the quality of your experience.

Booking flights and accommodations well in advance can result in significant savings. Traveling during the UK's off-peak seasons, such as late autumn and winter, also allows you to avoid peak prices and the busiest crowds.

Opt for public transport wherever possible to save on travel costs. In cities like London, purchase an Oyster card or use contactless payments to access the cheapest fares. If you plan to travel extensively by train, consider buying a Railcard, which offers a third off rail fares.

Instead of splurging on luxury hotels, consider staying at budget hotels, hostels, or using platforms like Airbnb to find more affordable accommodation options. Look for accommodations in areas just outside of major cities to get better deals while staying within easy reach of the main attractions.

Many museums, galleries, and parks across the UK offer free entry. Take advantage of these opportunities to explore the country's rich culture and history without spending a fortune. Even iconic landmarks like Buckingham Palace or Big Ben can be enjoyed from the outside without the need for paid tours.

Many UK supermarkets offer affordable meal deals for lunch, which typically include a sandwich, drink, and snack for under £5. Pubs also often have special offers on certain days of the week, with affordable prices for traditional British meals like fish and chips or bangers and mash. Opt for a filling pub lunch and save fine dining for special occasions.

Purchase discount cards like the London Pass or National Trust Membership, which give you access to discounted or free entry to a wide variety of attractions across the UK. These cards can help you save significantly if you're planning to visit multiple locations during your trip.

Currency, Tipping, and Handling Money in the UK

Understanding how to handle money in the UK will help you navigate your expenses smoothly. The local currency is the British pound sterling (£), and while credit and debit cards are widely accepted, it's always good to carry some cash for smaller purchases or in rural areas where card payments may not be available.

Before your trip, it's wise to exchange some money to have on hand for immediate expenses like taxis or snacks. You can exchange currency at banks, airports, or currency exchange services, though it's best to avoid airport exchange booths as they often charge higher fees. Alternatively, use ATMs in the UK to withdraw pounds directly, as this often results in better exchange rates, though your home bank may charge international transaction fees.

Tipping in the UK is generally more reserved compared to the United States. In restaurants, it's customary to leave a tip of 10% to 15% if service is not already included in the bill. In pubs, taxis, and casual eateries, tipping is not required, though rounding up to the nearest pound or leaving small change is appreciated.

Credit and debit cards, especially contactless payments, are widely used in the UK, even for small purchases. It's convenient to use cards for most transactions, but having some cash is useful in rural areas, markets, or for small tips. Apple Pay, Google Pay, and other mobile payment methods are also accepted in many places.

If you're using an international card in the UK, be aware of potential foreign transaction fees. Some cards offer fee-free international use, so consider applying for one before your trip. Always choose to pay in the local currency when offered the option to pay in pounds or your home currency, as this will often result in a better exchange rate.

By carefully planning your budget and using smart travel strategies, you can enjoy everything the UK has to offer while keeping your costs in check. From finding affordable flights and accommodations to making the most of public transportation and local dining options, a well-planned budget will help you experience the UK in a cost-effective way, without missing out on any of its cultural richness or natural beauty.

CHAPTER 11

Practical Tips and Advice for Your UK Journey

Traveling to the United Kingdom is a remarkable experience, filled with opportunities to explore rich history, stunning landscapes, and vibrant cities. To make the most of your trip, it's essential to be well-prepared with practical tips that ensure a smooth and enjoyable journey. From safety and health precautions to understanding local customs and the weather, being informed will help you feel more confident as you navigate this diverse and dynamic country.

Safety and Health Precautions

The UK is generally considered a safe destination for travelers, but like any other country, it's important to stay aware of your surroundings and take basic safety precautions. In major cities like London, pickpocketing can occur in crowded tourist areas, so always keep an eye on your belongings and avoid displaying valuable items like cameras or phones unnecessarily. Using a cross-body bag or money belt can offer extra protection against theft.

When it comes to health, the UK's healthcare system is one of the best in the world, and as a visitor, you can access medical care through the National Health Service (NHS) for urgent situations. However, it's recommended to have comprehensive travel insurance that covers both health and travel-related issues such as lost luggage or trip cancellations. Most pharmacies, known as "chemists" in the UK, are widely available in cities and towns, so over-the-counter medications can be easily accessed.

In terms of vaccinations, there are no mandatory vaccines required for entering the UK. However, it's always a good idea to ensure your routine vaccines are up to date, especially for measles, mumps, rubella (MMR), and influenza, as these are common in many regions of the world.

If you plan to explore the countryside or engage in outdoor activities such as hiking, it's important to be aware of changing weather conditions. Carry a basic first aid kit and ensure you have the proper gear, especially in more remote areas like the Scottish Highlands, where access to medical facilities might take longer.

Etiquette and Customs

The British are known for their politeness and adherence to social norms, so familiarizing yourself with a few local customs will help you blend in and show respect for the culture. Greeting someone with a simple "hello" or "good morning" is standard, and when addressing people in a professional or formal setting, it's customary to use titles such as "Mr." or "Ms." followed by the last name, unless invited to use first names.

Queueing is a deeply ingrained part of British culture. Whether you're waiting for a bus, at a supermarket checkout, or entering a venue, forming a line (or "queue") and waiting your turn is expected. Jumping the queue is seen as rude and inconsiderate.

When visiting British homes, it's polite to bring a small gift such as flowers, wine, or chocolates. You should also remove your shoes if invited inside, especially in rural or suburban areas where homes may be carpeted.

Tipping practices in the UK are more reserved than in some other countries. In restaurants, tipping between 10% and 15% is appreciated if service is not already included in the bill. Tipping is not usually expected in pubs or casual eateries, though rounding up your bill is a nice gesture.

Public behavior tends to be relatively reserved, particularly in comparison to more expressive cultures. It's best to keep your voice down in public spaces like buses, trains, or restaurants. Additionally, when riding public transportation, offering your seat to the elderly, disabled, or pregnant women is a common courtesy.

Language, Weather, and Time Zones

Although English is the official language of the UK, the country is home to several regional languages and dialects. In Wales, Welsh is widely spoken alongside English, and road signs are often bilingual. In Scotland, you may hear Scots Gaelic, especially in the Highlands and the Outer Hebrides, while in Northern Ireland, some locals speak Irish Gaelic. While most people speak English fluently, learning a few basic Welsh or Gaelic phrases can be a nice gesture when visiting these areas.

Weather in the UK can be unpredictable and varies significantly by region. The country is known for its frequent rain, especially in the west and northwest, so always carry an umbrella or waterproof jacket. Winters can be cold, with average temperatures around 1–7°C (34–45°F), while summers are mild, typically ranging between 15–25°C (59–77°F). If you're traveling in autumn or spring, layering your clothing is the best way to adapt to sudden changes in temperature.

The UK follows Greenwich Mean Time (GMT) in the winter months and switches to British Summer Time (BST), which is GMT+1, during the summer. This daylight saving time usually starts in late March and ends in late October. Be mindful of this change, especially if you're traveling in the spring or fall, to avoid any confusion with flight or train schedules.

Because the UK is relatively far north, daylight hours can vary greatly depending on the time of year. In summer, you can expect long days, with daylight lasting until 9 or 10 p.m., especially in Scotland. Conversely, winter days are much shorter, with darkness falling as early as 4 p.m. in December. These seasonal changes can impact your plans for sightseeing and outdoor activities, so be sure to check local sunrise and sunset times.

Staying Connected

Staying connected while traveling is important for navigation, communication, and researching local attractions. Most of the UK has reliable mobile network coverage, and you can easily purchase a local SIM card if your phone is unlocked. Mobile providers like Vodafone, EE, and O2 offer prepaid options that include data, calls, and text, often at a reasonable cost. Alternatively, you can use international roaming, but be sure to check with your home provider for rates.

Free Wi-Fi is widely available in cafes, restaurants, hotels, and even on public transport in some cities like London. Major cities and tourist areas often offer public Wi-Fi hotspots, but these may not be as common in rural or remote regions.

Emergency Numbers and Contacts

In case of emergency, dial **999** or **112** to reach police, fire services, or medical assistance. These numbers are toll-free, and operators can connect you to the appropriate service. If you need non-urgent medical advice, you can call **111** for help with minor illnesses, finding a local doctor, or advice on how to access healthcare services.

It's always a good idea to keep a list of important contacts handy, including your embassy or consulate, insurance providers, and emergency contacts from home. Being well-prepared ensures that you can quickly resolve any issues that may arise during your travels.

By familiarizing yourself with these practical tips and advice, you'll be well-equipped to enjoy a smooth and memorable journey through the UK, embracing its unique culture while staying safe and well-prepared for any situation that might come your way.

Here's a breakdown of what each emergency service covers:

- **Police:** For any crime in progress, threats to safety, or public disturbances, contact the police.

If you are the victim of theft, assault, or vandalism, the police can assist and file reports.

- **Ambulance:** For urgent medical emergencies, such as severe injuries, sudden illness, or life-threatening conditions, an ambulance can be dispatched to your location.
- **Fire Services:** If there is a fire, a gas leak, or any other dangerous situation involving hazardous materials, the fire services should be contacted immediately.
- **Coastguard:** For emergencies at sea or along the coast, including boat accidents, stranded individuals, or drowning, the coastguard can provide search and rescue assistance.

It's important to note that the UK's emergency services are well-coordinated, so if a situation requires more than one service (for example, an accident involving a fire and injuries), the operator will ensure the appropriate services respond.

Non-Urgent Medical Assistance: NHS 111

For medical situations that are not life-threatening but still require advice or guidance, the UK provides a free helpline through **NHS 111**. This service is available 24/7 and can help with a wide range of health concerns, such as minor injuries, fevers, cold and flu symptoms, or questions about medications. NHS 111 can also direct you to local healthcare services, including pharmacies, walk-in centers, and out-of-hours doctors, if needed.

The NHS 111 service is particularly useful if you are unsure whether you need to visit a hospital or seek medical treatment. The trained professionals who answer the calls will ask you questions about your symptoms and recommend the best course of action, which may include self-care advice, a GP appointment, or a referral to a hospital or urgent care center.

Embassies and Consulates

For travelers, it's essential to have the contact details of your country's embassy or consulate in case of passport issues, legal concerns, or other matters that require diplomatic assistance. Embassies and consulates can offer a wide range of services, including issuing replacement passports, providing guidance on local laws, and offering support during emergencies such as natural disasters or civil unrest.

Embassies are usually located in the capital, London, while consulates may be found in major cities such as Manchester, Edinburgh, and Cardiff. In the event of a serious legal or personal emergency, your embassy can also help liaise with local authorities and provide necessary support.

Before you travel, make a note of the following details for your country's embassy or consulate:

- The address, phone number, and website of the embassy.
- Any emergency contact numbers for after-hours assistance.
- Email addresses for non-urgent queries.

You can often register your trip with your embassy before you travel, which allows them to contact you in case of emergencies affecting your region, such as natural disasters or significant security threats.

Important Travel Insurance Contacts

Having comprehensive travel insurance is highly recommended when traveling to the UK, as it provides protection against unexpected medical bills, lost luggage, trip cancellations, and other unforeseen issues. In case of an emergency, such as a medical evacuation or hospitalization, your travel insurance provider will be a critical resource.

Make sure to keep a copy of your travel insurance policy, along with the following key information:

- 24-hour emergency assistance hotline for your insurance provider.
- Your policy number and any relevant reference codes.
- Procedures for filing claims and necessary documentation.

It's also a good idea to familiarize yourself with what your insurance covers before your trip. For example, some policies might include coverage for extreme sports or adventure activities, while others may require additional riders for certain high-risk activities like skiing or hiking.

Local Health Services and Pharmacies

In addition to emergency services, it's useful to know about local health facilities in the UK, especially if you need non-urgent care during your trip. In larger cities, you will find numerous **NHS walk-in centers** that offer treatment for minor injuries, illnesses, and urgent but non-life-threatening conditions. These centers do not require an appointment and can be a convenient option if you need medical assistance outside regular GP hours.

Pharmacies, commonly known as **chemists**, are widely available throughout the UK and provide over-the-counter medications, first aid supplies, and general health advice. In large cities, chains like **Boots** and **Superdrug** offer extended hours, while smaller independent pharmacies may have more limited opening times. It's a good idea to ask your hotel concierge or a local resident where the nearest pharmacy is located, especially if you're staying in a rural area.

Keeping a Personal Emergency Kit

To ensure you're prepared for minor issues, it's worth carrying a small personal emergency kit during your travels. This can include:

- Basic first aid supplies (bandages, antiseptic wipes, pain relievers, etc.).
- Any prescription medications you regularly take.
- Travel-sized toiletries, sunscreen, and insect repellent.
- A list of emergency contacts, including family members, your embassy, and your travel insurance provider.
- Copies of important documents like your passport and insurance policy.

Being prepared with these emergency numbers and contacts will not only give you peace of mind during your travels in the UK but will also enable you to respond quickly and effectively should an emergency arise. Whether you encounter a health issue, need to report a crime, or simply require advice, knowing who to contact ensures that you're never far from the help you need.

CHAPTER 11

Sustainable Travel in the UK

Sustainable travel is becoming an increasingly important consideration for tourists worldwide, and the United Kingdom is no exception. With its rich landscapes, vibrant cities, and unique cultural heritage, the UK offers travelers an opportunity to explore responsibly while minimizing their environmental impact. Traveling sustainably isn't just about reducing your carbon footprint—it's also about supporting local communities, preserving the environment, and respecting cultural traditions. By following eco-friendly travel practices, you can enjoy a fulfilling and conscious journey through the UK.

Eco-Friendly Travel Tips

To minimize your environmental footprint while traveling through the UK, making conscious decisions regarding transportation, accommodations, and daily activities is essential. One of the most effective ways to travel sustainably in the UK is to rely on the extensive public transportation network. The UK is home to a highly developed rail system that connects major cities, towns, and even remote areas. Trains are an excellent option for reducing carbon emissions compared to cars or domestic flights. Long-distance train services, such as the ones operated by National Rail and Great Western Railway, are efficient and comfortable, offering a scenic way to explore the countryside and urban landscapes.

For getting around within cities, options like buses, trams, and the London Underground offer a sustainable alternative to taxis or rental cars. Biking and walking are also popular and eco-friendly ways to explore many UK cities. London, for example, has invested heavily in cycling infrastructure, and bike-sharing schemes such as Santander Cycles are available in many urban centers.

When it comes to accommodation, many hotels, bed-and-breakfasts, and hostels in the UK are adopting eco-friendly practices. Look for establishments that prioritize sustainability by using renewable energy, offering locally sourced food, or participating in green certification programs. Many eco-conscious accommodations have been recognized by organizations like Green Tourism, which helps travelers find places committed to reducing their environmental impact. Small efforts like reusing towels, limiting energy consumption, and recycling can make a big difference when staying at any property.

Another way to reduce your environmental footprint is to minimize plastic waste. Carrying a reusable water bottle and avoiding single-use plastics like disposable cutlery or straws will help decrease waste during your trip. Tap water is safe to drink throughout the UK, and many cafes and public spaces offer free water refills. Opting for reusable bags when shopping is another simple way to cut down on plastic waste.

For those who want to go even further in offsetting the carbon emissions from their travel, many carbon offsetting programs allow you to invest in environmental projects. These initiatives, such as reforestation efforts or renewable energy developments, help neutralize the emissions produced during your trip, making your journey more environmentally responsible.

Supporting Local Communities

Sustainable travel isn't just about environmental conservation; it's also about supporting the people and cultures that make your destination unique. In the UK, there are countless opportunities to contribute positively to local economies and foster connections with communities.

Shopping locally is a fantastic way to support artisans, farmers, and small businesses across the UK. Many towns and cities are home to markets where you can find handmade crafts, local produce, and unique souvenirs that reflect the culture and traditions of the region. For example, places like the Cotswolds, Yorkshire, and Cornwall are known for their artisan markets, where you can purchase handcrafted items ranging from pottery and textiles to locally produced food. By buying from these markets, you're directly supporting local craftsmanship and reducing the environmental impact of mass-produced goods.

Dining at locally-owned restaurants and cafes is another excellent way to give back to the communities you visit. The UK boasts a diverse food scene, with locally sourced ingredients often taking center stage. Whether you're enjoying traditional fish and chips by the seaside or sampling regional delicacies like Cornish pasties, dining locally helps small businesses thrive and ensures that your money stays within the community. Rural areas, in particular, benefit greatly from travelers who choose family-run establishments, as these businesses are often integral to the local economy.

For those looking to engage more deeply with the local culture, participating in community-based tourism initiatives is a rewarding way to travel. Some regions in the UK offer immersive experiences where you can connect with local residents, learn traditional crafts, or participate in community events. This type of tourism not only fosters cultural exchange but also helps sustain small, rural communities that may otherwise be overlooked by mainstream tourism.

Traveling Responsibly

Responsible travel in the UK involves making thoughtful decisions that ensure both the preservation of natural landscapes and the respect for cultural heritage. One key aspect of responsible travel is to respect historical and cultural sites. The UK is home to some of the world's most famous landmarks, including Stonehenge, Edinburgh Castle, and the Tower of London. When visiting these sites, it's essential to follow guidelines, stay on designated paths, and refrain from touching or climbing on ancient monuments to help preserve them for future generations.

Another important aspect of responsible travel is respecting wildlife and natural habitats. The UK is known for its diverse ecosystems, ranging from coastal regions teeming with birdlife to forests home to endangered species like red squirrels. When exploring these areas, be sure to stick to established trails, avoid feeding wildlife, and follow the guidance of park rangers and conservationists. If you're interested in wildlife watching, choose eco-certified tours that prioritize conservation and animal welfare.

Overtourism can have a detrimental effect on popular destinations, especially during peak travel seasons. To combat this, consider exploring lesser-known areas or traveling during the off-season. The UK is full of hidden gems that provide just as much charm and beauty as the more well-known spots. For example, while cities like London and Edinburgh are popular, exploring smaller towns such as Bath, York, or Canterbury offers a quieter, more intimate experience while reducing pressure on heavily touristed areas.

Lastly, adopting the "Leave No Trace" principle when exploring the UK's natural beauty ensures that you minimize your environmental impact. Pack out all waste, avoid picking plants or disturbing wildlife, and leave areas as pristine as you found them. This is particularly important in national parks like the Lake District or the Scottish Highlands, where tourism can strain delicate ecosystems.

By embracing sustainable travel practices, supporting local communities, and respecting the natural and cultural heritage of the UK, you can enjoy a more enriching and eco-conscious journey. Sustainable travel not only benefits the environment but also helps ensure that future generations can experience the same beauty and wonder that makes the UK such a special destination.

Itinerary Tips for Sustainable Travel in the UK

When planning a sustainable trip across the UK, creating an itinerary that balances environmental considerations, cultural exploration, and efficient travel is key. Here are some tips for crafting an eco-friendly, enriching itinerary that allows you to experience the best the UK has to offer:

1. Plan Around Public Transportation

One of the easiest ways to make your trip more sustainable is to utilize the UK's excellent public transport system. The extensive rail network connects major cities and scenic regions, so building your itinerary around train routes can reduce your reliance on cars or flights. When possible, opt for direct routes to minimize carbon emissions, and explore regions that are well-served by buses and trains, such as the Lake District, the Cotswolds, and Scotland's Highlands.

- **Tip:** Use rail passes like the BritRail Pass, which allows unlimited travel on trains, making it easier and more affordable to explore multiple regions by train.

2. Prioritize Longer Stays in Each Location

To reduce the environmental impact of frequent travel, plan to stay in each destination for several days rather than moving to a new location each day. This not only cuts down on transportation emissions but also allows you to immerse yourself more deeply in each place, giving you time to explore beyond the typical tourist sites.

For example, you might spend a few days in the culturally rich cities of London, Edinburgh, or Bath before heading to more remote areas like the Isle of Skye or the Cornish coast. Slowing down your itinerary can also reduce travel fatigue and allow for a more relaxed experience.

3. Explore National Parks and Nature Reserves

The UK is known for its breathtaking natural landscapes, and spending time in national parks and nature reserves is both environmentally friendly and rewarding. Places like the Lake District, Snowdonia, and the Peak District offer fantastic hiking, wildlife watching, and eco-friendly outdoor activities. Many of these parks are accessible by public transport, making it easier to travel sustainably.

When visiting rural or natural areas, stick to marked trails, respect wildlife, and avoid leaving any waste behind. Choose eco-friendly accommodations in these areas, such as eco-lodges or sustainable guesthouses, which often prioritize renewable energy and water conservation.

4. Visit Off-the-Beaten-Path Locations

To avoid overtourism and explore areas that are less crowded, consider adding lesser-known destinations to your itinerary. Smaller towns, villages, and rural areas often offer just as much charm as more famous spots but with fewer crowds and less environmental pressure.

For example, instead of focusing solely on London, consider visiting smaller cities like York, Cambridge, or St. Andrews. In Wales, places like Brecon Beacons or Pembrokeshire offer beautiful scenery and fewer tourists than hotspots like Snowdonia. Similarly, in Scotland, the

Outer Hebrides or the Orkney Islands provide stunning natural beauty without the influx of visitors seen in more popular areas.

5. Support Local Businesses and Sustainable Tours

As you travel, look for opportunities to support local businesses by choosing locally owned restaurants, shops, and tour operators. You can also research sustainable tours that emphasize low-impact travel and contribute to conservation efforts. These might include guided wildlife tours, walking or cycling tours, or eco-friendly cruises in areas like the Scottish isles or along the Jurassic Coast in England.

Many local businesses are committed to sustainability, whether by sourcing local, organic food or offering unique cultural experiences that engage with and support local communities.

6. Book Accommodations in Central Locations

When choosing where to stay, opt for accommodations that are centrally located in cities or towns. This allows you to explore much of the destination on foot or by bike, reducing the need for cars or taxis. Staying in the city center of places like London, Bath, or Edinburgh provides easy access to cultural attractions, restaurants, and public transportation hubs.

Many UK cities are highly walkable, and staying in central locations allows you to experience the destination more intimately, whether it's by wandering through historical streets, visiting local markets, or enjoying nearby parks.

7. Time Your Visit to Avoid Peak Tourist Seasons

Traveling during the off-season is another way to practice sustainable tourism, as it reduces the strain on popular destinations. Visiting in spring or autumn instead of summer allows you to enjoy milder weather, fewer crowds, and often lower prices for accommodations and attractions.

Certain events and festivals are worth timing your visit for, but be mindful of the environmental impact that larger events can have on the local infrastructure. When planning around festivals like Glastonbury or Edinburgh Fringe, be sure to book eco-friendly accommodations and plan transportation well in advance.

8. Combine Cities and Nature for a Balanced Experience

For a well-rounded itinerary, consider combining time spent in bustling cities with outdoor adventures in nature. This allows you to experience both the cultural richness of urban areas and the tranquility of the countryside, all while reducing the environmental impact of excessive urban travel.

For example, after spending a few days in London or Edinburgh, you could head to nearby natural escapes like the Cotswolds, the Highlands, or coastal towns in Cornwall or Northumberland. This variety offers a fulfilling experience while balancing urban energy with the calm of nature.

9. Pack Smart for the UK's Variable Weather

Packing efficiently and appropriately for the UK's ever-changing weather is key to reducing the need for buying extra gear or wasting resources. Layered clothing, a waterproof jacket, and reusable items like water bottles and shopping bags are essentials for eco-conscious travelers. By packing versatile items, you can reduce waste and minimize your need to purchase additional supplies during your trip.

10. Be Flexible and Open to Spontaneous Experiences

While it's helpful to have a general plan, remaining flexible can lead to unexpected discoveries and lower your environmental impact. You might find that traveling by train to a lesser-known village or spontaneously joining a local event offers a more meaningful experience than sticking strictly to your original itinerary.

Being open to these moments can make your journey more sustainable by allowing you to explore at a slower pace and immerse yourself in local life, rather than rushing through a checklist of must-see attractions.

By following these sustainable travel tips and crafting a thoughtful itinerary, you can enjoy a rewarding and responsible trip through the UK that leaves a positive impact on the places you visit.

Best Travel Apps for Exploring the UK

When traveling through the UK, there are numerous travel apps that can enhance your experience, simplify logistics, and help you travel more sustainably. Here are some of the most useful travel apps for getting around, finding accommodations, discovering attractions, and managing your itinerary in the UK:

1. Citymapper

Citymapper is a must-have app for navigating major cities in the UK, including London, Manchester, Birmingham, and Edinburgh. It provides real-time information on public transportation options like buses, trains, trams, and even bike routes. The app also offers detailed maps, step-by-step navigation, and estimated travel times for walking, cycling, and rideshare services. Citymapper is especially helpful for tourists who are new to navigating the UK's public transport system, and it also shows eco-friendly travel options.

2. Trainline

For exploring the UK by train, Trainline is an essential app. It allows you to search for and book train tickets for travel across the UK, including journeys between cities and rural destinations. You can view train schedules, check live departure and arrival times, and receive notifications about any delays or disruptions. The app also compares prices to help you find the best deals, and you can often save money by booking in advance. Additionally, Trainline supports mobile tickets, reducing the need for printed paper.

3. National Trust and English Heritage Apps

These apps are perfect for history buffs and nature lovers who want to explore the UK's heritage sites, stately homes, gardens, and castles. Both the **National Trust** and **English Heritage** apps provide detailed information about thousands of historical sites across the UK, including opening hours, entry fees, and nearby attractions. The apps also include offline maps, making them great for areas with limited mobile service. With these apps, you can explore iconic locations like Stonehenge, Hadrian's Wall, and the beautiful gardens of National Trust properties.

4. Google Maps

Google Maps remains one of the best all-around travel apps for navigation and discovering attractions. It offers turn-by-turn directions, public transit routes, walking and cycling paths, and real-time traffic updates. The app is invaluable for navigating both urban and rural areas in the UK, finding local restaurants, cafes, and shops, and exploring landmarks. You can also download offline maps of specific areas in case you're traveling without access to data.

5. Airbnb

If you're looking for unique places to stay, **Airbnb** is a great app to find accommodations, ranging from city-center apartments to countryside cottages and even castles. The app allows you to book a wide range of properties directly from local hosts, many of which offer eco-friendly features like energy-efficient homes or properties built with sustainability in mind. Airbnb also has an **Experiences** feature, where you can book local tours, workshops, or cultural activities hosted by locals.

6. Skyscanner

For finding affordable flights within and to the UK, **Skyscanner** is a top choice. The app allows you to search for and compare flights from different airlines, offering a variety of filters to help you find the best prices, eco-friendly options, and shortest travel times. Skyscanner also includes options for booking hotels and car rentals, making it a versatile tool for travel planning. You can set price alerts to track flight prices and get notified of the best deals.

7. Rome2Rio

Rome2Rio is an excellent app for figuring out how to get from one place to another, especially if you're traveling between different regions of the UK. The app provides information on all available modes of transportation, including flights, trains, buses, ferries, and car rentals, along with their associated costs and travel times. Rome2Rio is particularly useful for planning multi-leg journeys and finding the most eco-friendly routes, such as train and bus travel over domestic flights.

8. XE Currency

If you're visiting the UK from abroad, **XE Currency** is a great app to help you keep track of exchange rates and manage your budget. It allows you to convert currencies on the go and provides real-time exchange rate updates. XE Currency can also store offline rates, which is helpful when you're in areas with poor internet connectivity. This app is particularly useful if you're traveling between the UK and other European countries and need to manage multiple currencies.

9. TripIt

TripIt is a comprehensive travel organizer that helps you keep track of all your travel details in one place. Once you book flights, accommodations, and activities, you can forward your confirmation emails to TripIt, and it will automatically create a detailed itinerary for you. The app also offers reminders for check-in times, gate changes, and other essential details, helping you stay organized while traveling across the UK. With TripIt, you can also access maps and directions for each segment of your journey, even offline.

10. Good Pub Guide

For travelers wanting to experience authentic British pubs, the **Good Pub Guide** is an app that helps you find the best pubs across the UK. The app includes detailed reviews, location maps, and suggestions for pubs based on user ratings. Whether you're in search of traditional pub food, craft beers, or a cozy atmosphere, this app is an invaluable resource for finding hidden gems throughout the country.

11. UK Weather Apps (BBC Weather or Met Office)

The UK's weather can be unpredictable, so having a reliable weather app is crucial. **BBC Weather** and the **Met Office Weather** app are both excellent options for real-time weather forecasts, alerts, and detailed information on rain, wind, and temperature. You can check the weather for specific cities or regions, which is especially helpful when planning outdoor activities like hiking in national parks or walking along the coast.

12. Green Travel Apps

For eco-conscious travelers, there are apps like **Giki Zero** and **Joro** that help you track your carbon footprint and suggest ways to offset it. These apps provide tips on reducing your environmental impact during travel by choosing sustainable transport, accommodations, and activities. They also allow you to measure the carbon emissions from your trip and offer suggestions for offsetting through environmental projects.

By utilizing these travel apps, you can streamline your trip, save money, and make more eco-friendly choices while exploring the UK. Whether you're navigating the streets of London, finding the best pub in a small village, or booking a last-minute train ticket, these apps will enhance your travel experience.

Conclusion

As your adventure across the United Kingdom draws to a close, it's time to reflect on the remarkable journey you've just experienced. From the bustling streets of London to the serene landscapes of the Scottish Highlands, and from the rich historical sites to the hidden gems of rural England, the UK offers an unparalleled diversity of experiences. Whether you were captivated by the vibrant cities, enchanted by the history and culture, or rejuvenated by the natural beauty, your journey has undoubtedly left you with a treasure trove of memories.

The UK is a place where modernity and tradition blend seamlessly. It's a destination where you can stroll through centuries-old castles in the morning and enjoy cutting-edge theatre in the evening. This balance of the old and the new is one of the country's greatest strengths, offering travelers a truly unique experience that is both enriching and inspiring. Every region has something distinct to offer, whether it's the rugged coastlines of

Wales, the rolling hills of the Cotswolds, or the cosmopolitan energy of cities like Manchester, Glasgow, or Cardiff.

Leaving with Memories and New Insights

As you prepare to leave, you'll find that the UK has given you not just wonderful memories but also a deeper understanding of its cultural heritage, its people, and the land itself. The stories you've collected, the food you've tasted, and the people you've met all combine to create a tapestry of experiences that will stay with you long after you've left.

Travel often broadens our perspectives, and the UK is a destination that allows for profound connections—whether through its rich literary history, diverse music scenes, or simple, heartfelt conversations in a countryside pub. You may have started the journey with a set of expectations, but undoubtedly, the real experience has given you more than you could have imagined. The warmth of the people, the beauty of the landscapes, and the intriguing complexity of British life may inspire you to return someday.

As you reflect on your journey, consider how the insights you've gained can enrich not only your life but also those around you. Share your stories, your newfound knowledge, and your appreciation for the history, culture, and landscapes of the UK. Encourage others to explore the hidden gems, support sustainable tourism, and approach travel with curiosity and respect for local traditions and communities.

Sustainable Travel Practices for the Future

One of the most important lessons from traveling is the responsibility we carry as global citizens. By making environmentally conscious choices during your journey—whether through using public transportation, supporting local businesses, or minimizing waste—you've played a role in ensuring that future travelers can continue to enjoy the beauty of the UK. Sustainable travel is more than just a trend; it's a way to preserve the places we love while respecting the communities and ecosystems that make them special.

As you plan future adventures, continue to prioritize responsible travel habits. Whether returning to the UK or exploring new destinations, the practices you've adopted will help make travel more enriching for everyone involved.

In conclusion, your journey through the UK has not only provided unforgettable moments but has also deepened your understanding of a country that is both steeped in history and constantly evolving. It's a place where the past informs the present, and where every traveler can find something that resonates deeply with them. As you leave, take with you the knowledge, experiences, and memories that have made your trip to the UK an adventure of a lifetime. And remember, the door is always open to return. The UK's beauty, culture, and history are timeless, waiting to welcome you back whenever you choose to visit again.

Acknowledgments

Creating this travel guide to the United Kingdom has been a journey in itself, and it would not have been possible without the support, guidance, and inspiration of many individuals and organizations. I would like to take this opportunity to express my heartfelt gratitude to everyone who contributed to the success of this project.

First and foremost, I want to thank the countless travelers and locals who shared their stories, experiences, and tips. Your insights added authenticity and depth to this guide, offering a genuine perspective on what it's like to explore the UK. To those who generously opened their homes, businesses, and communities to visitors, I extend my appreciation. Your warm hospitality is what makes travel through the UK so memorable.

Special thanks to the various tourism boards and visitor centers across the UK, including **VisitBritain**, **VisitScotland**, **VisitWales**, and **Discover Northern Ireland**. Your dedication to promoting sustainable and authentic tourism has been an invaluable resource in shaping this guide. The wealth of information, from detailed maps to insider recommendations, helped ensure that readers can experience the UK to its fullest.

I'd also like to acknowledge the countless historians, tour guides, museum curators, and experts who helped bring the rich history and cultural heritage of the UK to life. Your passion for preserving and sharing the stories of the past is deeply appreciated, and I hope this guide reflects the incredible work you do in making history accessible to travelers.

To my dedicated team of researchers and editors, your tireless efforts in gathering information, refining details, and ensuring accuracy were essential to the creation of this guide. Your keen eye for detail and commitment to quality were crucial in delivering a professional and polished resource for readers. Thank you for your hard work and dedication.

A big thank you to the local restaurants, hotels, and businesses who shared their expertise and recommendations. Your willingness to provide tips on everything from regional delicacies to unique accommodations has added richness to the guide, allowing travelers to experience the UK like a local.

Lastly, to my readers and fellow travelers—thank you for your continued support and enthusiasm. It is your curiosity, love of exploration, and desire to discover new places that make guides like this possible. I hope this book inspires you to set off on your own adventures, uncover hidden gems, and create lasting memories in the UK.

With deepest gratitude, I dedicate this guide to all those who love to travel, learn, and explore.

Appendix

The appendix provides essential information that will enhance your travel experience in the United Kingdom. Whether you're looking for important contacts, detailed maps, or suggestions for further reading, this section aims to equip you with practical tools to ensure your journey is as smooth and enriching as possible.

Useful Contacts and Resources

Having access to reliable contacts and resources is invaluable when traveling, especially in a diverse and vast country like the UK. Here is a list of important contacts to keep in mind during your trip:

- **Emergency Services**: Dial **999** or **112** for police, ambulance, or fire services.
- **Non-Emergency Police**: Dial **101** for non-emergency police matters.
- **National Health Service (NHS)**: Dial **111** for non-emergency medical advice.
- **UK Visitor Information Centers**:
    - **VisitBritain**: +44 (0)20 7578 1000
    - **VisitScotland**: +44 (0)131 332 2433

- - VisitWales: +44 (0)370 556 0560
  - Discover Northern Ireland: +44 (0)28 9023 1221
- **British Consulate Services:**
  - London: +44 (0)20 7008 1500
  - Edinburgh: +44 (0)131 556 8466
- **Airports:**
  - London Heathrow (LHR): +44 (0)844 335 1801
  - Manchester Airport (MAN): +44 (0)161 489 8000
  - Edinburgh Airport (EDI): +44 (0)131 348 4203

In addition to these contacts, it's always helpful to research local contacts specific to your itinerary, such as hotel numbers, tour operators, and any relevant embassy contacts if traveling internationally.

Maps of the UK

Having access to a variety of maps is crucial when exploring the UK, whether you're navigating through bustling cities, discovering the beauty of national parks, or traversing the charming countryside. There are several options for both digital and physical maps:

- **City Maps**:

    For navigating cities like London, Edinburgh, or Manchester, you can use apps like **Google Maps** or **Citymapper** for digital navigation. Physical maps of cities are also available at most visitor centers and tourist offices.

- **Regional and Country Maps**:

    For traveling between regions or exploring rural areas, **Ordnance Survey Maps** are highly recommended. They offer detailed maps for hikers, cyclists, and adventurers. You can also purchase physical maps at most bookshops or outdoor gear stores.

- **Driving Maps**:

    If you're renting a car, having a reliable driving map is essential. **AA Route Planner** and **Michelin Maps** are widely used for detailed road maps and routes throughout the UK.

Many travelers also opt to download offline maps via **Google Maps** to ensure they have access to navigation tools even when they lose cell service.

Recommended Reading and Further Information

The UK's rich history, culture, and landscape make it an ideal destination for curious travelers who want to delve deeper. Here are some recommended books and resources for further reading that will enhance your understanding of the UK:

- **"Britain by the Book" by Oliver Tearle**: A journey through Britain's literary history, exploring the places that inspired famous British authors.
- **"The Wild Places" by Robert Macfarlane**: A beautifully written exploration of the UK's most remote and wild landscapes.
- **"Notes from a Small Island" by Bill Bryson**: A humorous and insightful travel memoir that captures the unique charm of British life and culture.

- **"The Rough Guide to the UK"**: An in-depth travel guide offering detailed recommendations for places to visit, accommodations, and cultural insights across the country.
- **National Trust Guidebooks**: These provide detailed historical and cultural insights into the most famous and beloved heritage sites throughout the UK.

For more up-to-date resources, travelers can also refer to online travel blogs, government tourism websites, or audio guides specific to certain regions or attractions.

Frequently Asked Questions (FAQ)

1. What is the best time to visit the UK?
The UK can be visited year-round, but the best time depends on your preferences. Spring (March to May) and autumn (September to November) offer mild weather, fewer crowds, and vibrant landscapes. Summer (June to August) is popular for festivals and outdoor events, though it tends to be busier. Winter (December to February) is ideal for travelers seeking holiday markets,

cozy pub experiences, or visits to iconic cities like London without large tourist crowds.

2. Do I need a visa to travel to the UK?

Visa requirements depend on your nationality. Citizens from the European Union, the United States, Canada, Australia, and New Zealand typically do not require a visa for short-term tourist stays. However, it's always advisable to check with the **UK government's visa and immigration website** before planning your trip.

3. What is the best way to get around the UK?

The UK has an excellent public transportation system, with trains, buses, and subways (particularly in London). **Trains** are a convenient way to travel between cities, while buses and subways are great for local transit. Renting a car is a good option if you plan to explore rural areas like the Scottish Highlands or the Lake District.

4. Is tipping expected in the UK?

Tipping is not mandatory, but it is appreciated. In restaurants, a 10-15% tip is typical, unless a service charge is already included. For taxi drivers, rounding up to the nearest pound is common. Hotel staff and tour guides also appreciate small tips for good service.

5. What currency is used in the UK?
The currency in the UK is the **British Pound Sterling (GBP)**. While credit and debit cards are widely accepted, especially in cities, it's advisable to carry some cash for smaller purchases, especially in rural areas or markets.

6. What is the weather like in the UK?
The weather in the UK can be unpredictable, with rain possible at any time of year. Summer temperatures range from 15-25°C (59-77°F), while winter temperatures can drop to 0-10°C (32-50°F). Always pack layers and be prepared for rain, particularly if you're visiting in the autumn or spring.

7. Can I use my mobile phone in the UK?
Yes, most international mobile phones will work in the UK, but you may incur roaming charges. It's recommended to check with your service provider before traveling. Alternatively, you can purchase a **local SIM card** or use **Wi-Fi** for data.

8. Is the UK safe for tourists?

The UK is generally very safe for tourists. However, as with any destination, it's wise to stay aware of your surroundings, particularly in crowded places or tourist areas where pickpocketing can occur. Emergency services are highly responsive, and you can dial **999** in case of any issues.

This appendix aims to ensure you have all the practical information you need, from contact numbers to maps and essential resources. Armed with these tools, you'll be ready to explore the UK with confidence and ease!

Printed in Great Britain
by Amazon